Tunes, Tarts and Travel-itis

Eighteen Years of Facts, Faces and Fun with the Alex Welsh Band

JIM DOUGLAS

INTRODUCTION

Jim Douglas was born in the village of Gifford, near Edinburgh, in May 1942. Showing an early musical ability on violin and later drums, he acquired a guitar in 1957 to join the popular skiffle craze at the age of fifteen. On hearing the British traditional jazz revival, with such bands as Ken Colyer and Chris Barber, his musical path was soon headed in that direction. In the same year, while still at school, he formed a jazz band, 'The Hidden Town Dixielanders', with fellow student, clarinettist, Pete Kerr. The band was soon successful and led to a winning appearance in the 'Carrol Levis Discoveries' competition, resulting in a prize of a trip to London to record on BBC radio's 'Workers' Playtime'. Going from strength to strength and after changing their name to 'The Capitol Jazz Band', the band appeared for two months in German jazz clubs in December, 1960. On their return, due to differences of opinion as to whether to become professional or stay amateur, they disbanded. Pete, followed shortly by Jim, joined the famous 'Clyde Valley Stompers', where they were happy for eighteen months. After a policy disagreement with the management, the entire band left and Pete formed 'The Scottish All Stars', which again only lasted a short time.

Back in London, after a few months of unemployment, Jim joined The Alex Welsh Band, with whom he was happily employed for eighteen years, until the bandleader's untimely death in 1982.

ACKNOWLEDGEMENTS

I would like to dedicate this book to the brave souls, some no longer with us, who suffered my presence on the bandstand, at the bar, in the wagon, home and abroad, Summer, Spring, Autumn and Winter for eighteen wonderful years. I would also like to thank my wife, Maggie and son, Will for their encouragement and patience while I undertook the writing of this labour of love and the many fans of the band who have waited so long for me to finish it, who I hope are reading this now.

Also special thanks to Pete Skivington for the photographs, Adam Croft and Peter Kerr for their encouragement and advice, and Libby Calaby for her help in the final editing and formatting.

CONTENTS

JIM DOUGLAS

CHAPTER ONE

A FISHY BEGINNING

I t can't be easy to play the guitar when your fingers are sticky with latex rubber adhesive. Not that I ever found out, because I was hardly playing at the time.

The year was 1962, and after tasting stardom for eighteen months or so with a good band called The Clyde Valley Stompers, my career seemed to be *rocketing to oblivion*, as the saying goes. I was sharing a dismal room and kitchen with fellow Scotsman and drummer, Billy Law, in 'desirable' Alexandra Park Road in Muswell Hill, North London. We had both been fired from the 'Stompers' organisation for asking for what we, along with the other members of the band, thought to be a rightful wage, considering the amount of gigs we had. We had lost our digs in upmarket Finchley, where we had rented a couple of rooms from an Irish alcoholic doctor, who had spent several years at sea and in the Far East; he had specialised in venereal diseases and now shared his life with a bisexual girlfriend and a crazy Kerry Blue, after his wife had had enough of the *arrangement* and left him.

We were, to be euphemistic, *freelancing*. In other words, we were trying to make a go of it in the jazz business, at a time when the jazz business was also trying to make a go of it, and, because of the R&B craze, everyone was failing miserably.

Although his furnishings were Spartan, our landlord was Greek. He had just enough command of the English language to convey to me that, unless I was willing to work in his shoe factory to earn enough money to pay my part of the rent, he would deprive us of the cosy squalor in the dirty, freezing shit-house, in which we lived. Billy's financial contribution came from his eligibility to draw the dole every week and the odd gig he managed to pick up. To be fair, my job was reasonable, if menial, with enough payment to keep Mr Grab-the-lot-opoulos off our backs and offer some creature comforts, like the occasional flagon of cider.

Most Sunday evenings, the Alex Welsh Band played at The Fishmongers' Arms pub in Wood Green, a mere half-hour walk from our digs. Naturally, we found ourselves visiting this jazz oasis in our musically barren desert more and more regularly. We would time our arrival to just before the band was due to take the stand and would quaff a swift half in the saloon bar in the hope that someone would invite us in to save our entry fee because we were broke. I relied on my hero, Diz Disley, who had temporarily re-joined the band after guitarist, Tony Pitt, had left. But, alas, he was often conspicuous by his absence and I had to find alternative means of gaining admittance.

One night, the answer came quite unexpectedly. I had vaguely known Alex from my days with The Clydes, and was quite well acquainted with drummer, Lennie Hastings, who had deputised for us on a couple of recordings. But, I was not

11

prepared, one halcyon evening, for the words, "Have you got your guitar, laddie?" coming from the direction of the band leader.

I didn't wait for him to change his mind. Cadging a lift from a friend, I raced back to our digs to pick up my instrument. Euphoria is not just a state of mind; it is the reality of playing in the best band in the land, in a damp, atmospheric, freezing cold, acoustically disastrous brick extension, to a typical Victorian North London pub on a bleak winter's Sunday evening.

As I have briefly mentioned, 'trad jazz' had reached its nadir by this time. Due to agents cashing in on the success of the likes of Barber, Bilk and Ball, second-rate, pantomime copies had flooded the business. Amateurs, semi-professionals and professionals alike, had joined or formed 'trad' bands and were, at the whim of their agents, mimicking their heroes by donning fancy outfits and adopting thematic names, such as 'Storeyville Gamblers', 'City Gents', or even 'New Orleans Knights'. In their efforts to look the part, most of the musicians forgot about the music and the inspirational heroes they were supposed to love. They had built their careers around an effort to reach stardom through the hit parade, abandoning jazz standards and substituting 'trad' versions of popular tunes from other musical media. The airwaves were flooded with the wailing of squeaking clarinets, arse-ripping farting trombones, and plonking, tinny banjos. One famous promoter, Roger Horton of the '100 Club', or 'Jazzshows', as it was known then, is attributed to having remarked, "Show me a banjo and I'll show you a profit."

That summed it up nicely. It came to a head with the introduction of a band dressed as Southern State Confederates, complete with war wounds, bandages, arms in slings, and the bass transported like a coffin, draped with the Confederate flag. (Somehow they all mysteriously healed themselves, when the necessity to play arose.) At the end of the gig, the re-adorned bass was transported out the room to the strains of 'John Brown's Body', or so I am reliably informed.

Throughout all this nonsense, Alex Welsh steadfastly held on to his musical principles and tastes. Although not gaining the financial rewards and acclaim he deserved, his reputation for playing quality jazz was intact, and his supporters stayed loyal to him in much the same way as those of Ken Colyer, Bruce Turner, Chris Barber, and Humphrey Lyttelton.

By 1963, most of the agents had abandoned the sinking 'trad' ship in favour of the rhythm and blues packets that were cruising the musical seas. Beatlemania was in its infancy and the Liverpool sound whispered on the horizon. The 'trad boom' was as dead as a dodo. Alex, together with the aforementioned Ken Colyer, Terry Lightfoot, and Monty Sunshine, suddenly found themselves without gigs. Forced to find their own engagements, they managed, with the help of loyal promoters, such as Ken Lindsay and Steve Duman, to set up a little circuit of clubs and pubs around Greater London that were willing to take jazz bands. The idea was to follow each other around this circuit, playing the same venue every four or five weeks or so, and creating enough venues to have three or four gigs per week. This became affectionately known as doing the 'milk round'.

The theme repeated itself all over the country. Jazz clubs were suddenly R&B dives, so that with notable exceptions (such as the Manchester Sports Guild, Birmingham's Digbeth Civic Hall, and The Dancing Slipper at West Bridgeford, Nottingham), the jazz scene all but dried up.

After my exhilarating début that wonderful evening at the Fish, I was invited to join the band every Sunday (without official payment, although Alex used to slip me a couple of quid for 'expenses'). For obvious economic reasons, Alex had decided to resort to a three-piece rhythm section for most of the band's gigs. I found myself being asked to do more and more, however, and one day, Alex said, "Look, laddie, you may as well do all the gigs, for what they're worth. Welcome to The Alex Welsh Band."

A couple of weeks or so went by and I soon realised, however, that it wasn't an entirely happy ship I had embarked on. There was constant bickering among the guys, especially after a drink or two, which had, on a couple of occasions before I joined, led to a half-hearted exchange of blows. After one particular gig at the Rex Cinema in Cambridge, a real ding-dong had broken out. Maybe it should have been called the Wrecks Cinema, because Merrydown Cider, (an extremely potent libation that was not widely available), was sold at the pub nearby. This was a magnet to a jazz musician; it is also incredibly mood enhancing.

The club itself was unlicensed to sell alcohol, which always led to rather serious over-imbibing during the break, and probably a small carry-out in the pocket. The evening in question was no exception. After an ordinary performance with its usual bickering, the band had set off home, quietly sipping at their travelling comforters. All was peaceful. Suddenly, Alex received a blow to the side of the head, delivered by a silently seething Roy Crimmins. All hell broke loose, as other frustrations among the chaps were turned into punches. Pianist, Fred Hunt, who was driving, pulled the bus to a halt and everyone disembarked, but the mood was over and, after some token swinging of fists, everyone re-took their seat and quietly dropped off.

The next day, Alex was sporting a black eye, Lennie's head had a few unusual lumps, and a sore-fisted Roy was full of remorse and embarrassment. *Gloria sic transit mundi!* (There's no glory to be gained from fighting in a band bus on a Monday morning!) The next evening saw three deputies in the band.

The second round was between Len and 'wouldn't hurt a fly' Bill Reid. Travelling back together from Ipswich after a gig, they decided to stop for a bite to eat at an all-night transport café. While eating, a disagreement led to an argument. Getting more and more heated, they decided to settle the matter outside. One blow from ex-matelot Bill and the affair was over. They went back to their nosh and drove home as if nothing had happened.

Some months later, when Archie Semple was too infirm to continue playing, Alex invited Al Gay to join the band.

"I'd love to," replied a wary Al, "but I can't fight."

He joined anyway and, with the exception of Fred Hunt, (who had left to follow a solo career elsewhere and had been replaced by ex-Clyde Valley Stomper, Kirkcaldy-born Bert Murray, and Tony Pitt, (who was considering a career as a pop star), this was the line-up I joined: Alex on cornet; Roy Crimmins, trombone; Al Gay, sax and clarinet; Bert Murray, piano; Bill Reid bass, and Lennie Hastings, drums. This lasted for about six weeks until suddenly, after an Alex Welsh Big Band concert at Exeter University, Bert was fired.

I had played with Bert with the Clydes, so I knew just what he could be like. When sober, he acted like an angel and could be a lot of fun, but if he had been drinking, he was a belligerent little sod, who niggled and complained all the time, incessantly moaning about the way the band played, and insisting on the correct (his) approach to arranging the band's repertoire. I had learned to accept and handle his cussedness during our time together in the Clydes, by appearing to accept his foibles and agreeing with him. I had even enjoyed some very pleasant Sunday afternoons, with lunch and a few drinks, while listening to his favourite music, in the company of his lovely wife and childhood sweetheart, Marion, and their poodle, Heather. I listened to his musical theories, and indeed learned from them, finding them to be of considerable substance and value. But, it was his biting sense of humour that stays with me to this day, and several famous remarks he made will endure forever:

"If you want to know the time, Oscar Peterson!" and, "Somewhere there's music, och aye, the noo!"

Well worth repeating before moving on, are a couple of anecdotes, often repeated among musicians:

The legendary guitarist, Barney Kessel, was appearing at the '100 Club'. He had just started to play Johnny Green's lovely ballad, 'Body and Soul', and the room was silent. Suddenly, from the direction of the entrance stairway, a voice was heard singing, "Barney put the Kessel on, Barney put the Kessel on." Bert had arrived! Approaching the bar, he was heard to remark, "I bet he gets the middle eight wrong."

A few moments later, with the guitarist a few bars into the middle eight, the silence was once again interrupted by Bert: "WRO-O-ONG!" he loudly yelled.

The other reminiscence, is that, on the occasion when Bert stayed overnight at the home of Jeff Green, the fine guitarist, on being awakened in the morning by Mrs Green, bearing a cup of tea, the hung over musician opened one eye and enquired, "Is there any whisky in it?"

To the bemused lady's negative reply, Bert querulously responded, "What's the story behind that, then?"

The best story of all, however, happened in the quiet Bedfordshire hamlet of Westoning, one summer evening in 1962. Bert, together with vibraphonist, Roger Nobes, was following a Jaguar car, being driven at a fair speed to a party laid on for the band after their local gig. As they approached the double bend, which serves as a High Street in Westoning, Bert lost control of the Hillman Husky estate car he was driving. In the centre of the village, bang on the road, there is a thatched-roof pub, The Chequers, which had survived all adversities, including Goering's bombing campaign during the Second World War, and was the focal point of the area.

With a, "...So, anyway, I said to this fellow!" directed to his passenger, Bert drove straight into the Lounge Bar, destroying it completely. The whole of his car was in the pub. The landlord slept through everything, only being awakened by the sound of an approaching fire engine. Roger came off worst, severing his larynx as he went through the windscreen, but Bert merely cut his thumb. A couple of weeks later, the incident made the headlines in the local press:

'DRUNKEN SCOT ACHIEVES WHAT LUFTWAFFE FAILED'

But I digress. Bert had obviously outstayed his welcome, and hearing a rumour that Fred Hunt wanted his old job back, I suppose he inevitably had to go. Sometime later, after many escapades and adventures, including being banned from every country in South Africa with trumpeter, Bob Taylor, Bert ironically joined The Temperance Seven, with whom he spent several happy years, until his untimely death from a heart attack while riding his bike home from a lunchtime gig.

No sooner had Fred settled back into the rhythm section than it was the turn of bassist Bill Reid to decide to quit. To be fair, Bill had been contemplating his future for some time, and had more or less planned a new life as a pig farmer. He was the most unassuming member of Alex's band, but from what I remember, had quite a lot of influence (based on good sense), on the running of the band. I know for a fact that he was responsible for a lot of the financial matters.

A smallish man, with a slightly-too-large cranium, crowned by greying, wiry hair, Bill was short-sighted, necessitating the wearing of thick, rimless spectacles. He was cruelly known as 'The Fly', because of his slight resemblance to the subject of the film of the same name.

Bill's sense of humour was dry and witty, and could be taken the wrong way if you didn't know him. When I joined, he was living with his charming wife, Jackie, in a bungalow in Bushey, Hertfordshire. He christened me 'Auld Reekie' after the capital of Scotland, from where I had moved south. I hit it off with him pretty well and we often travelled to gigs together in his mini-van. I was sorry to see him go. It seemed to me that all my heroes were departing at the same time. He was going to be difficult to replace.

Diz Disley, Brenda Gower, Jean Hunt, Archie Semple, Alex, Sue Semple, Roy Crimmins, Jackie Reid; and in front, Fred Hunt and Len Hastings. Camera man, Bill Reid

Author with ventilated pedal extremities

CHAPTER TWO

THE TWO RONNIES

For a few months before leaving the Clyde Valley Stompers, I had been joined in the rhythm section by a young bassist from the Shetland Isles, by the name of Rognvald Mathewson, or Ron for short. (Several people still remember their Norwegian ancestry in name and customs in Shetland *vis a vis* the Festival of *'Up Helly Aa'* in which a Viking long ship is burned.)

It should also be mentioned that Ron had a brother, Harald, who became known as jazz pianist, 'Matt' Mathewson. I had some recordings that Ron and I had made together as part of Pete Kerr's Capitol Jazz Band, formed on our return to

Scotland and employing the majority of the 'sacked' Clyde Valley Stompers. With the help of these recordings, I managed to persuade Alex to give Ron a trial. He got the job, of course, and he and I set up home in a flat in West Kensington. This necessitated my moving out of the famous rooms in Fawley Road, which through the years had housed among others, Sandy Brown, Brian Lemon, Keith Ingham, Colin Purbrook, Billy Law, and Tony Baylis. (I first met bassist, Dave Green, in Fawley Road; on returning from a gig in the middle of the night, I found him fast asleep in my bed. 'Fall-out Road' was a bit like that.)

Ronnie Mathewson learned to play the bass by watching someone else. The capital town of Lerwick boasted a dance band with (unusual for that period) a bass player in its ranks. Every weekend they played in the local dance hall where a teen-aged Ron would stand in front of the band watching every move the bassist made. One fateful night, probably through too much *uisquebaugh,* the unfortunate fellow was indisposed and had to leave the bandstand.

'I can play that bass!" piped up young Rognvald.

"Well, you better get up here and show me," answered the indulgent band leader.

Ron did...and he could! Within six months of that evening he was as good as anyone I knew.

At his birth, it was discovered that Ron's left eye had an incurable problem, and it was removed and replaced by an artificial one. As he grew, his false eyes were adjusted

23

accordingly, so by the time he was an adult, he had several which he kept in a little plastic container. As you will imagine, they became the source of great amusement and the butt of many jokes; either as props, or used as puns, to his less than tactful colleagues, in the various bands to which he added his considerable talent. The unblinking, staring, offensive articles would find themselves in Chinese food ("Waiter there's an eye in my Chop Suey!"), at the bottom of half-empty beer glasses, and even once inserted inside a certain part of Ron's anatomy to portray a 'one-eyed trouser snake'. Best of all, they were used to help construct a grotesque face consisting of Lennie Hastings' toupee, two of Ron's eyes, my upper denture, and a tomato for a nose.

Song titles became: The Knight has a Poisoned Eye; Eye Society; Please Don't Talk About Me, One Eye's Gone; and Ma, He's Made an Eye at Me. Ron accepted all of it with a great sense of humour and dignity.

Because of his Shetland upbringing, Ron at first portrayed a degree of naïveté. Still a self-confessed virgin at nineteen, he was desperate to become a man, in the fullest sense of the word. This is how it eventually happened: The 'Clydes' were booked to play in the Olympia Ballroom, Reading, one of the less appetising venues on the 'trad' circuit. From what I can remember, the Army was in town that evening and the club was full of soldiers. During the interval, Ron had latched on to a girl, who had already had some dealings with some of Her Majesty's

Forces. Either still frustrated, or unsatisfied, she took Young Lochinvar backstage and introduced him to the sins of the flesh.

Back on the stage, the interval over: no Ron.

"Where the hell is he?" demanded Pete Kerr.

Half way through the second number, a red-faced Ron rejoined the band.

"Where the hell have you been?" asked Pete.

"I've done it! I've done it!" replied the breathless bassist. "I've had if off at last, and I can prove it! I'm still wearing the Johnny!"

Thank goodness for Y-fronts.

Sometime later, we were living in a rented house in East Finchley, North London. Trying to get gigs in a rapidly dying jazz scene was proving harder and harder; we were more-or-less existing on dole cheques and parcels from home. One night, after we had found some dosh from somewhere or another, we took a trip up-West. On the late tube home, Ron picked up a none-too-clean-looking 'scrubber'. We warned him off.

"What about these blemishes on her legs?"

"If you must know, they're dog bites," our hero replied.

The inevitable happened: Gonorrhoea.

Ron had been seeing a very nice girl called Pat, and when he discovered his affliction, we insisted he should inform her. I remember it, because it was the day John F. Kennedy died. Everyone remembers where they were on that fateful afternoon. Ron picked up the phone and dialled Pat's number.

Maybe we shouldn't have been eavesdropping, but we wanted to be sure she was informed of his infection.

"Isn't it awful about Kennedy?" Ron opened.

On and on he went for about twenty minutes, talking mostly about the Kennedy affair.

"And, by the way," he said, "I've got the pox," and he put the phone down.

When Ron wasn't chasing ladies or actually playing with the band, he was sleeping; during daylight hours, that is. We had by this time, moved lock, stock and instruments into my mother's house in the beautiful village of Gifford, in the Parish of Yester, East Lothian. God knows how she managed to feed and sleep another five of us, but feed us and sleep us, she did. I remember we always liked to treat her to a Sunday drink in the local bar of the Tweeddale Arms Hotel. If you remember, the licensing laws were such that, in Scotland only hotels could serve alcohol on the Sabbath, and only between the hours of 12.30pm to 2.30pm, and 6.30pm to 10.00pm. One particular afternoon about two o'clock, we were all in the pub except for Ron, who was in bed. My Uncle Jake, who was more like a brother to me, and definitely one of the chaps, suddenly said, "Maybe someone ought to ring home and see if Ronnie wants a drink before they close?"

Someone did, and a breathless, sleepy-eyed wreck arrived in the bar with about ten minutes to go. Getting himself a pint, he sat down at our table next to a friendly farmer and his snoozing, faithful border collie. Suddenly, with a howl of anguish, the dog leapt up, soaking wet from muzzle to tail. Ron had taken one sip from his pint and immediately fallen asleep where he sat, emptying his pint pot all over the wretched animal.

Number 20 Stanwick Road, West Kensington, was not unlike Fawley Road, inasmuch as it was tenanted mostly by professional musicians, actors and the like, as it happened, from Australia or New Zealand. Ron and I rented the top floor consisting of a living room, bedroom and kitchen, with a communal bathroom / toilet half a floor below, which we shared with two New Zealand air hostesses. The ground floor housed a couple with whom we had little or no contact, while the basement was occupied by three Australian girls, one of whom was the celebrated lead singer of the famous New Seekers, the lovely Judith Durham. Don't forget that this was the swinging-sixties. I remember parties nearly every weekend in one flat or the other. On returning from a gig, even in the middle of the night, it would be no surprise to find something going on somewhere, especially over the weekend.

By now, Ron was a fully paid-up member of the Non Virgin Society, and seemed to be doing his best to get on to the Board of Directors' table. I wasn't as pure as the driven snow either, but didn't belong in his league, finding myself either sleeping alone in the bedroom, or alternatively, on the sofa in the lounge.

Eventually I found Ron sleeping all day, and I took to playing golf more and more just to get out of the flat. On my return, Ron would still be in bed and the place would be a shambles. One day the landlady came for the rent, took one look at the place, and gave us a week's notice. I moved in with some friends just around the corner in Lisgar Avenue, while Ron took a room in a house full of modern jazz musicians in Sinclair Road, where he still resides to this day.

Musically of course, the band benefited from his playing. With the return of Fred Hunt, the rhythm section, driven by the wonderful Lennie Hastings, settled into a powerful, swinging unit, reminding listeners of a more American approach. Al Gay and Roy Crimmins had moved on, to be replaced by the superb multi-instrumentalist, John Barnes, and the phenomenal Roy Williams, both of whom added different colours to the band and new material to the repertoire. We had toured the country with several famous Americans, and received enthusiastic notices for our performances everywhere we went. Alex thought it was time to make an album, and having been approached by Acker Bilk's brother David, we went into the studios to cut 'Strike One' for his newly formed company.

A couple of years before, we had had a session with Wild Bill Davison, recorded by Jazzology, for the American market. At the time of writing, these two recordings are all we have of Ron's time with the band, but they are wonderful examples of his talent; especially the former. (Other un-issued tapes have been discovered since then and are currently being issued on several labels.)

Soon after, looking for something a bit more demanding than Dixieland / Mainstream, Ron left to join Fat John Cox's band for a tour of Holland. He was to return to us briefly a few months later.

"Are there any more like him up there in Scotland?" Alex had asked me on accepting Ron's notice to quit.

"I know of another Ron, maybe not such a good technician, but nevertheless a fine steady player. His surname's Rae, and he lives in Musselburgh."

"We had better try him then," Alex replied.

Once again the Band struck lucky.

Although his approach to playing the bass was different to the flamboyant Shetlander's style, Ron Rae adopted a more head down, dig-in method; he fitted the rhythm section to a T.

I had two beds in my room, one of which he gratefully occupied while looking for a rented house for his wife, Margaret, and their four or five children. He could be described as stocky and balding, although only a few years older than me. Ex-plumber, Ron Rae, also had the reputation of being a bit of a hard man. I believe this reputation had been derived from a short fuse to his tinder box temper, allied to the fact that he couldn't stand musical inadequacy, especially if he had to be part of it, playing in some of the lesser bands in and around Edinburgh.

Most of the time he wore a broad grin on a mouth which he frequently opened wide to emit a loud joyful laugh. The chaps in the band took to him immediately, as did the American visitors with whom we were still involved in tours; notably the wonderful cornettist, Ruby Braff, particularly enjoyed his time and tone.

For a few weeks everything was coming up roses again. But, rain clouds were unfortunately just beyond the horizon. Ron's wife, Margaret, hated both London and the new lifestyle she had been asked to accept. The kids, with their broad Scottish accents, were bullied at school, and the house they had rented was next to a pig farm on the periphery of Heathrow Airport. The unhappiness of his family, the pungent porcine pong, and the ear-shattering roar of the jet engines became too much to accept. Knowing that Ron Mathewson was back in London looking for work, Ron Rae packed his family back off to Musselburgh, gave Alex notice, and left, a very disappointed man.

So the Viking returned, and for a few months everything was *Valhalla* for him. Inevitably (we knew it wouldn't last), his more modern musical brain tired of humble Dixieland once again. Ron's friend, the extraordinary pianist, Mike Pyne had joined the wonderful Tubby Hayes, who was also looking for a bass player. Who better than Ron? With all our good wishes for his future, he once more left the band; this time we knew it was for good.

For the next twenty years or so, our paths crossed spasmodically, usually by chance. After Tubby's premature death, Ron joined Ronnie Scott's fine band, staying for many years until his own health, due to excessive living, enforced his departure. He doesn't play anymore and has become a recluse. Still a young man, he is in a very poor state of health and I fear the worst for him.

Would the 'Double R Man' come back? The reply was to the affirmative. (Alex had a bosom buddy called Laurie Ridley, who gave us all nicknames. I was known as 'Wee Hoots', John was 'Boko Banana', Roy became 'Royston Carnforth De Vere Merryweather Williams', and Tony Baylis became 'Boney Tailess', and eventually 'Napoleon'. He even included himself, signing his birthday cards, 'Riddle the Yiddle!' appertaining to his Jewish birth right.)

There was still a room going at Lisgar Terrace, which Ron Rae acquired for a few weeks, before we both moved to Mornington Avenue, numbers 2 and 20 respectively; both basement rooms. He gave up any ideas of moving his family southward – an arrangement agreeable to both him and his wife – and once more settled into the band for what was probably its most musically productive period.

Ron had spent his period away from the band, working with the harmonically superb pianist, Alex Shaw, in Edinburgh, and brought the knowledge he had gleaned from the master with him. He owned a small Gibson Cromwell guitar, on which he arranged tunes for the band. 'The Shadow of Your Smile' was his, as were 'Shiny Stockings' and 'Girl Talk'.

We spent most of our free time together, listening to recordings and puffing a little pot occasionally. Bix Duff, the Scottish pianist, who was staying with me at this time (he had asked to be put up for a couple of nights and was still with me six months later), took an afternoon gig with clarinettist, John Evans, in a drinking club in Hammersmith, and we went there often. It wasn't long until regular little sessions took place there. Drummer, Don Cook, turned up regularly and Ron and I would take our axes along for a blow. Don introduced us to an Aberdonian lady, with whom Ron struck up an immediate close friendship. An inevitable affair started between them, getting more and more serious for Ron. I don't intend to spend long, writing of the guys' moralistic eccentricities. Better to acknowledge that certain things, as in all walks of life, did take place, but belong in the past and in the personal memories of the people involved.

I am breaking my rule to tell of Ron's indiscretion, only because it was directly responsible for his leaving the band for the second and final time. I think he felt he was getting in over his head and the only option left was to return to Scotland, and to his wife and family. So departed, in my opinion, one of the best bass players I ever played with, and certainly the most suited to the band that Alex ever employed.

Chapter Three

Rhode Island Ready

I'm afraid I've gotten ahead of myself. Now, where was I? Ah yes: The Milk Round!

With Ron Mathewson's arrival, Alex once again had a settled band. All we needed were engagements. The answer was just on the horizon. Apparently, the jazz scene in America was also in decline and stars were looking abroad for the income they had enjoyed in the States. Britain was one of the obvious countries they turned to. Wild Bill Davison arrived to tour with a makeshift Freddie Randall Band, and this set the ball rolling. A jazz fan in Manchester, Jack Swinnerton, approached his colleague L.C. Jenkins ('Jenks' to his friends), with the idea of using American guests in the basement bar of his Sports Guild. In conjunction with London agent, Jack Higgins, Jack Teagarden was approached. Unfortunately, the maestro was too ill to travel and his place was taken by the legendary trumpet player, Henry 'Red' Allen. Henry would appear at the Guild for four nights, accompanied by four different bands; Alex Welsh, Bruce Turner, Sandy Brown, and Humphrey Lyttelton, followed by a tour of the country. To accompany Henry on this two-to-three-week tour, Jack Higgins suggested The Alex Welsh Band.

During the next three or four years, the band undertook something in excess of twenty tours, backing American legends. Henry was followed by Pee Wee Russell, Wild Bill Davison, Earl Hines, Dicky Wells, Bud Freeman, Rex Stewart, Eddie Miller, Henry again, Wild Bill again, Ruby Braff, Peanuts Hucko, and then Henry 'Red' for a second, third, and last time. In between tours we went back to the normal round robin of clubs, pubs, and the occasional concert hall, but playing now to noticeably larger audiences.

As I have already recorded in a previous chapter, Alex decided to cut a few albums. The first was called 'Strike One', named for the reason that it was the first for a new company organised by Acker Bilk's brother David. The musical content – a mixture of the band's facets – was very satisfying and well presented by the chaps, but the production and pressing, in my opinion, left a lot to be desired. It has recently been cleaned up and re-produced by Lake Records as a CD, with a good deal of success. When it was first issued it caused a little bit of a storm. Typical reactions at its release, included: *Whose band is that? Are they American? Alex Welsh's? Don't be stupid, that's not a British band!*

It was, for Strike Records, alas, a one-day wonder. Apart from a companion sing-along type extended play record, I believe nothing else was ever produced. We received some great reviews from the musical press, and it sold quite a few copies, all of it doing the band no harm at all.

I remember meeting John Kendall (the manager of the second-hand department of Doug Dobell's jazz record shop in Charing Cross Road), for a drink shortly after its release, and he was raving about it. He told me that the shop was going to make it record of the month and feature it in the window. In Acker Bilk's Capricorn Club – an afternoon meeting place for chaps who fancied a tipple between opening hours – the bar's manager, Roy James (he had recently resigned from the banjo chair in Acker's band), played the record all the time. This naturally caused a little embarrassment, but also gave me an enormous sense of satisfaction when it was being played and I was present.

But in every rose bed, thorns sprout, and trouble was just around the corner. One of our regular engagements was on a week-night in the Corporation Hotel, Derby (it is no longer in existence, I'm sorry to say). Roger, the manager, had spent his years as a Regimental Sergeant Major in the forces in Germany. While there, he had developed a liking for German *gemutlichkeit*. Lennie and Roger became bosom buddies, sharing songs and experiences. He loved 'Auf wiedersehen', and the other Tauber take-offs. He was, I believe, also the source of some of the drummer's props. We were always all right at the Corporation for a swift half after the gig, while Alex did the business, but on the twenty fifth of January, 1967, it went too far. I can't remember whether there was some reason for celebration, but a full-blown party was going on in a side bar. There was a record player in operation with songs from the Munich Beer Festival bellowing from the speaker. We naturally joined in!

At dawn, we set off homewards. The transport still consisted of a car driven by Fred, but we had acquired a replacement for Len's van, a Thames mini-bus with side facing bench seats, handled by Roy. I travelled with Fred, Alex and Ron, leaving Len and John to accompany Roy with the equipment. I have no idea what time I got home. All I remember is being awakened by the telephone and a voice telling me that there had been an accident; three of the band were in hospital.

On the way home, on the M1 Motorway, Roy had started to feel a little tired and decided to make a stop at the services for a cup of coffee. Although only fifteen-to-twenty minutes away from his home in Luton, he didn't want to take the risk of falling asleep at the wheel. Unfortunately, that is exactly what happened. After leaving the café, the three weary musicians set off once more. About a mile or so down the road, Roy was awakened by the horn of a juggernaut, just in time to see the central reservation coming towards him. Instinctively, he yanked the steering wheel to the left. The top-heavy minibus rolled over, the near side front door flew open, and the passenger seat, with John still strapped to it, flew out of the vehicle, depositing the poor fellow face down on the hard shoulder. He suffered a fractured left cheek and collarbone, and damaged his teeth and jaw. Roy, still hanging on to the steering wheel, had his right ear nearly torn off, which later needed several stitches, while Len, sleeping through the whole episode, received minor burns from the acid contained in a spare battery, which had been stored near to him.

The van ended up against a signpost reading 'Junction 15'. Fortunately, the lorry driver had witnessed the whole business and immediately called for help. A short time later the three men, lucky to be alive, were taken to Luton and Dunstable Hospital. John was in a bad way. While the other two were kept in for a period of observation and later discharged (not before Len had donned the same clothes he had been wearing and got burned all over again), the clarinet player was dispatched to Mount Vernon to have his bones set and his face reconstructed. Fortunately, he was examined by a surgeon whose hobby was playing clarinet and he therefore received the best possible treatment, involving the manufacture of a tooth and gum shield to strengthen his weakened embouchure. John was out for three months. Al Gay, who in everyone's opinion is probably the most underrated musician around, and the wonderful Bruce Turner, handled his position in the front line. When John was well enough to play again, Al stayed on to enable the baritone player to recuperate his chops. Gradually Al's assistance was required less and less. Fortunately, there are a few albums around that were recorded with the eight-piece line-up, and they demonstrate what a big sound that front line had.

So things went on much as they had. Bass players came and went. We made a couple of trips to Europe. Germany was the most visited country, but we also appeared in Le Havre, and Barcelona, where top of the bill was Stan Getz. Our dates in the *Fatherland* were organised by an agent named Karl Heinz Lyrmann; a man with a dark sense of humour, who claimed he was responsible for having Mannheim destroyed by bombs in the last war, by falling asleep while on searchlight duty.

All the time American stars were still continuing to visit. A couple of expositions were organised, including one featuring guitarists Larry Coryell, Grant Green, George Benson, and Kenny Burrell, on the stage at the same time. The organiser of many of the visits, and director of the famous Newport Jazz festival, pianist, George Wein, brought over an all-star band, and better still some wonderful news for us; an invitation to appear at Newport on the next festival. The deal was this: because of work permit difficulties, the band would be invited to the festival as unpaid guests. In return for airfares and a week's free accommodation, plus peppercorn expenses, we would open the Saturday evening concert along with Pee Wee, Ruby, Bud, and Joe Venuti; one of my all-time heroes.

Of course, we jumped at the chance! Apart from the obvious personal prestigious satisfaction involved, just think of the publicity we would get as the first British band of its kind ever to appear at the Blue Riband Festival. So July 1968 saw us winging across the Atlantic Ocean to Boston, Massachusetts. It was a long flight, six hours or so, but with the aid of a couple of good books, a large rise in our adrenaline level, and the company of Arthur Bell, it passed quickly enough.

As soon as we touched down, the fun started. Having reclaimed our instruments and luggage we set off through Immigration and Customs Control. The officers were stopping and searching everyone. It seems that an hour or two before our flight landed, a young woman had been discovered carrying heroin, and the officials were on their toes. I immediately feared the worst. Len smoked a little pot now and again, but not the large spliffs made from three or more cigarette wrappers. His personal smokes were tiny little one-paper jobs, which he carelessly stuffed into his breast pocket to be rescued and re-used at a later date. If the Customs men searched him, we would be in trouble. When our turn arrived, we were given 'the works'.

"Who are you? What are you here for? Why do you have instruments with you? Do you have work permits?" the officials demanded. It wasn't made any easier by Len's laughing and joking as he gently mimicked the officials while he queued.

"All right you! Yes, you! Bring those drums through here."

They went through the drummer's equipment and luggage like a dose of salts. *Here it comes!* I thought, but to my relief and joy they let him pass. Fortunately his wife Jan had all his clothes dry-cleaned before his departure. All that the search had produced was a small black comb (moustache), and a cigarette card picture of Adolph Hitler.

After Alex produced a letter of explanation of our visit and an invitation to the festival, I was allowed to set foot onto American soil for the first time. In the arrival lounge, we were met by a road manager assigned to us for the duration of our visit, and, after stowing the luggage in a separate vehicle, we set off to Newport. I remember thinking as we drove through Massachusetts into New England, that it doesn't look much different to the countryside back home. Soon we arrived at our digs. We found them to be rooms in a dormitory of a girls' school, which of course was closed for the summer vacation, and set in its own grounds. Therefore we were afforded plenty of opportunity for practice without disturbing neighbours.

Due to the time difference, it was still early on the Tuesday morning when we arrived. We couldn't wait to see the festival site we had heard so much about and which had been the setting for the film, 'Jazz on a Summer's Day'. So, after a quick unpacking session and wash-and-brush-up, we were driven there.

The auditorium was a small fan-shaped field, large enough to accommodate something in excess of twenty thousand people. At the lowest point, where an imaginary handle might be, was a huge stage with its battery of microphones, and columns of speakers. Behind and under the platform were changing areas where the artists gathered and warmed up. Steps from the back entrance led up to the wings where the great Jo Jones had inspired Paul Gonsalves' famous twenty six chorus solo in 'Diminuendo and Crescendo in Blue', by tapping with a rolled-up newspaper.

As we rolled up and alighted, the first person we came across was Ruby, walking with a very familiar-faced man.

"Hi Alex! Hey do you cats know Woody? This is Woody Herman guys. Woody, these are the British cats I was telling you about."

And so it went on. We met Jo Jones, Dizzy Gillespie, Tal Farlow, and even the mighty Duke, although he was a bit too wrapped up in his own affairs to bother to spend time with us. He was, nevertheless, totally courteous on introduction.

I won't bore you with endless name dropping, however. Suffice to say we enjoyed a wonderful few days in the company of many of our heroes, listening to them, and joining them at parties. At one midnight party, I was thrilled to hear John and Roy play with Roland Kirk, while I chatted to Larry Coryell.

Saturday evening rolled around, and with it our performance. We were down to open the evening's proceedings with a short spell on our own, followed by our guests, individually and altogether for the last couple of numbers. I remember looking towards the audience as we began to play and thinking that they were a bit sparse for a Saturday evening, although numbering around three or four thousand. Of course, by the time everyone had been admitted and the sun had gone down half an hour later, there was a much bigger head count. I believe, by the time we finished, there were just fewer than twenty thousand bums-on-seats, or grass in this case. We opened with 'Dipper Mouth', then Alex sang something, probably 'Up a Lazy River', and John and Roy played 'Open Country' before we were joined by Pee Wee, Bud, Ruby and Joe Venuti, who got a standing ovation for 'Sweet Georgia Brown'. As a finale, Alex decided on the 'Royal Garden Blues'.

All the time we were playing, the next band on, the Duke Ellington Orchestra, were assembling in their seats behind us and quietly warming up together with the band. By the time we came to the last few choruses the whole orchestra had more or less joined in; what a sound! I still get goose bumps thinking about it. At the end of the final chorus, Len did his usual 'Oolyah, oolyah' four bar drum break before the whole ensemble rode out on a long ending. I looked round at the orchestra just in time to see Johnny Hodges nearly fall off his chair with laughter. The performance was widely acclaimed by

43

the American press. I have managed to save some of the reviews and they're reproduced here so that you can read them as they appeared.

The next, and in fact final day, was probably my most enjoyable (the festival excluded of course), of the entire week. It started with a lunchtime performance by the Ray Charles Orchestra, a few beers, a couple of hot dogs, and a glow from the night before. But the evening performance will remain in my memory forever. Count Basie was opening, then Dizzy Gillespie, and once more the Duke.

Just our luck, an assignation with a lady held up the driver assigned to take us to the concert, and we were going to be late for the start. At last, a little angry and frustrated, we arrived. As we got out we could hear something in the distance: Zhum! zhum! zhum! zhum! Suddenly it was followed by BA-DA-DAAA-DA! BA-DA-DAAA-DA! One by one we began running; even Alex with his dodgy leg. We arrived at the front of the stage to catch the last few bars of the Count, playing 'Shiny Stockings'. Wonderful!

The next day we left Newport to spend some hours in Boston prior to our return flight. We wandered around the streets for a while before calling into a bar for a short drink. The barmaid, intrigued by our accents, became very chatty and even presented Roy with a silver half-dollar as a keepsake. Killing time in a park before making our way to the airport and home, we discussed the festival and its implications. We fully expected in the light of the wonderful reviews, that we would go on to conquer the rest of the world. Unfortunately nothing much came from it, except the satisfaction of having been there, and the memory of one of the most unforgettable weeks in my life.

Roy Williams, Fred Hunt (hidden), Tony Baylis, Alex, Len Hastings, John Barnes, and me

THE NEWPORT JAZZ FESTIVAL
JULY 4, 5, 6, 7, 1968
Festival Field, Newport, Rhode Island

THURSDAY EVENING

July 4 at 8 p.m.

NINA SIMONE AND TRIO
CANNONBALL ADDERLEY QUINTET
COUNT BASIE ORCHESTRA
GARY BURTON QUARTET
JIM HALL
BARNEY KESSEL
MONGO SANTAMARIA SEPTET

SATURDAY EVENING

July 6 at 8 p.m.

DIONNE WARWICK
DUKE ELLINGTON AND ORCHESTRA
HUGH MASEKELA QUINTET
ALEX WELSH BAND AND GUESTS
    RUBY BRAFF
    BUD FREEMAN
    PEE WEE RUSSELL
    JOE VENUTI
AWARD WINNERS OF THE
    NOTRE DAME JAZZ FESTIVAL

SUNDAY AFTERNOON

July 7 at 2 p.m.

AN AFTERNOON WITH RAY CHARLES

FRIDAY AFTERNOON

July 5 at 2 p.m.

Buddy Morrow, The Clark Terry Big Band
Elvin Jones Trio, Archie Shepp Quartet

FRIDAY EVENING

July 5 at 8 p.m.

SCHLITZ SALUTE TO BIG BANDS
COUNT BASIE AND ORCHESTRA
DUKE ELLINGTON AND ORCHESTRA
DIZZY GILLESPIE ALUMNI BIG BAND
WOODY HERMAN AND ORCHESTRA
SPECIAL GUESTS: CHARLIE BARNET,
    TEX BENEKE, SONNY CRISS,
    ERSKINE HAWKINS, JACK LEONARD
Our thanks to the Jos. Schlitz Brewing Co.
for making this evening possible.

SUNDAY EVENING

July 7 at 8 p.m.

RAMSEY LEWIS
WES MONTGOMERY QUINTET
SPECIAL GUEST: FLIP WILSON
HORACE SILVER QUINTET
DON ELLIS ORCHESTRA
ROLAND KIRK
SOUND OF FEELING
AWARD WINNERS OF THE
    MONTREUX JAZZ FESTIVAL

SATURDAY AFTERNOON

July 6 at 2 p.m.

Duke Ellington with Johnny Hodges and
Buddy Carter, Horace Joe Squint
Tal Farlow Quartet, Sonny Criss, Vi Redd

Thursday, Friday, Saturday and Sunday Evening and Sunday Afternoon Concerts
$6.00, $5.50, $4.50 and $3.50. Box Seats $10.00 — All Seats Reserved

Friday and Saturday Afternoons — General Admission $3.00

All Programs Subject to Change

Accommodations

Many hotels, motels, rooming houses and private houses are
available in and around Newport. Write Newport County
Chamber of Commerce, Newport, Rhode Island 02840.

Travel To and From Newport

AIR — Scheduled airlines to Providence. Scheduled and by
request air taxi service to Newport.

BUS — Direct service from New York, Boston, Providence
and New Bedford.

TRAIN — To Providence from New York and Bus to Newport.

CAR — From Boston Route 138 to Bristol 24 to Fall River.
Follow signs to Newport. From New York Route 95 North to
138 East to R. I. 138. Follow signs to Newport.

PARKING ON FESTIVAL GROUNDS $1.00

ADDITIONAL NEWPORT FESTIVAL EVENTS

THE NEWPORT FOLK FESTIVAL, July 25-28. Evening Concerts — $6.00, $5.50, $4.50 and $3.50.
Daytime and Other Events $2.00 General Admission

BELAFONTE IN PERSON, July 29 Only $7.50, $6.25, $5.00 and $3.75

AN EVENING WITH ANDY WILLIAMS, August 3 Only — $7.50, $6.25, $5.00 and $3.75

HERB ALPERT AND THE TIJUANA BRASS, August 10 Only $7.50, $6.25, $5.00 and $3.25

Special Box Seats Available for All Events

Newport Daily News, Monday, July 8, 1968

London Band Opens Saturday's Jazz Festival

By JANE NIPPERT

CHAPTER FOUR

NICE

"All the boys were there.... Tony Parenti, Zutty Singleton, Joe Oliver, my man, Louis Armstrong, Kid Ory.... All the boys were there! I was right there with them! I hadda be; my fatha had the band!"

He breezed into my life like a galleon under full canvas, riding a mild zephyr. From his black patent leather shoes, upwards through exquisitely tailored trousers, bright red knitted shirt and beautifully cut mackintosh, to an elegant cheeky trilby hat perched on his head, he was immaculate.

Shining out from below the hat was one of the most intriguing countenances I had ever beheld. Here was a mahogany 'Idris lemon' (if you remember the advert), crinkly and warm, bisected by a full, fleshy mouth, smiling broadly and garnished with two big brown eyes that sparkled with unforgotten and anticipated mischief. Under this huge man's right arm nestled a trumpet wallet, dwarfed completely by the sheer size of the torso. As we were individually introduced, he answered with a monosyllabic, "Nice!"

The man, of course, was Henry 'Red' Allen Junior. The time was September 1963. The place was the Manchester Sports Guild. After a brief period of socialising over a pint of Younger's No.3 and a minimal rehearsal, we dispersed to await the evening performance. At this stage, I perhaps ought to admit that my feelings towards Henry were mixed. I had always erroneously associated him with the New Orleans mouldy fig style of jazz, but at the run-through, he had shown how wrong I had been; his playing produced new dimensions of which I had hitherto been totally unaware. I certainly wasn't prepared for what was to happen that evening.

*Ron Mathewson, Fred Hunt, Henry 'Red' Allen jnr, Alex Welsh,
Jim Douglas*

Arriving at the Guild after what became my routine whenever we visited Manchester (book into the hotel, bathe and shave, change into band uniform then set off to the Shambles for a nice steak and a tankard of real ale) I was amazed to see the place packed to the door so early. After exchanging pleasantries with friends and visiting critics and journalists, we took the stand. From what I can recall of that heady evening, I think we played a short set on our own, finally going into 'Way Down Yonder in New Orleans.' Half way through the first chorus came a sound and sight I'll remember forever. Rising above the band, Henry's trumpet soared as he made his way to the stand from the wings. I remember looking in the direction of the sound and seeing one of the most amazing visions I'd ever encountered; he looked magnificent!

Attired in a scarlet dinner jacket, black trousers, socks, and shiny shoes, his crinkly hair combed tight to his head, trumpet pointing to the ceiling, Red mounted the low stand. With a wave of a gold identity bracelet and a flurry of notes from his horn he ended the number.

"Again! Again! Here it is! Here it is!" he screamed over the applause, and went straight back into the same number. This time, after a few bars, he pointed to Roy Crimmins to solo. Like an orchestra conductor, as the solo came to a climax, Red once again stopped the band, but this time encouraging the trombonist to perform a cadenza.

"Nice! Make him happy, make him happy!"

He returned once more to the tune, pointing to a bemused Al Gay. The same formula followed, but this time after the applause, Henry took the solo bringing the number to an end with his own spine-tingling cadenza.

While we were still trying to regain our breath and control our adrenaline level, he called the next number, "Here's one! Here it is! The Canal Street Blues! Uh, uh, uh, uh!"

Off we went again. By now, the audience was going wild. Each tune performed in a similar style, almost like a mini work of art, featuring one or more of the band, or a vocal, which he delivered in his own inimitable way. Suddenly, it was my turn. I believe the tune was Earl Hines' 'Rosetta', but whatever it was I got the treatment. After a couple of choruses it was my turn for the cadenza. I don't think I had ever played a cadenza in my life before that evening, but somehow I managed. Then he started me again, same tune, same formula! My head was spinning, but somehow I coped. In fact I was out of myself looking in; you know the feeling.

"Make him happy! Make him happy! Nice!" Henry milked the audience and they did; I was quivering with excitement – my world would never be quite the same again.

For the next few evenings, Red was booked to play with Bruce Turner, Sandy Brown, and Humphrey Lyttelton's respective bands. I'm sure Henry changed their lives too, but I have a sneaky feeling not as much as ours. The next two weeks saw us on tour with the great man. I recall venues in Birmingham, Morden in Surrey, and the Rugby Club in Osterley Park, West London. One-armed Bill Kinell, 'Fu' to his friends, booked us into the Dancing Slipper at West Bridgeford, near Nottingham, where I believe the session was recorded privately.

By the end of the tour Henry and the band had become great friends, and with the help and the encouragement he and the press gave me, I felt I'd become twice the player I'd been. We were invited to record a television show for the Jazz 625 series at the Shepherd's Bush Theatre, in front of a live audience. Although our programme was obviously curtailed to incorporate as much variety as possible, some of the atmosphere was captured on the recording. I am pleased to say that, although much of the 625 series was scrapped, this one survives and is shown on BBC TV from time to time. It's a good recording and we are justifiably proud of it.

Red Allen with his 'final night' gifts

In all, we did four tours with Henry 'Red' Allen. He travelled in our less-than-comfortable transport, he stayed in our less-than-luxurious hotels, he dined with us in less-than-spotless transport cafes, and I never heard him complain once. He liked a beer; Younger's No 3 Scotch Ale and Newcastle Brown Ale were among his favourites. We presented him with an inscribed tankard as a memento of the first tour and he brought it with him on his return trips.

On his final tour, Henry was a shadow of his former self, suffering from incurable cancer of the pancreas, but his enthusiasm and energy remained undiminished. His last date with the band was in the Pheasant Inn in Carlisle. He had to leave the stand before the end of the concert, to catch a night train to London and his flight home in the morning. As he left, the tears were running down his cheeks; he knew we would never meet again. Two weeks later, he was dead.

I believe we were the last band he ever played with. Without exception, he was the most remarkable human being I have ever known.

Rest in peace, Henry Red. Make him happy! NICE!

For the next few months an anti-climactic feeling pervaded the band. To make matters worse, Al Gay had had enough and was about to leave to set up a nursing home in Windsor. After several auditions, including that of the wonderful Alan Cooper, who wasn't interested in being pro, and a very fine young PE teacher, Mike Schnelling, who decided to carry on in his vocational teaching career, the band was lucky enough to entice the brilliant multi-instrumentalist, John Barnes, from the Alan Elsdon Band, and the great Roy Williams from Terry Lightfoot to replace Roy Crimmins, who had decided to live in Germany. Their talents, along with their sense of humour and boyish pranks, kept us going in the humdrum routine of milk-round clubs, while at the same time widening the band's repertoire. They were of course present on the three remaining tours with Red, and at the start of – for me – the most musically rewarding years of the band's history.

CHAPTER FIVE

THE BAREFOOT BOYS

In the thirties, when one visited Belle Vue in Greater Manchester, one could be said to be literally 'going to the dogs'. The attraction of course was the greyhound racing. To the jazz world the place was much more important for something, or rather someone, who indeed was born there. I refer, of course, to John Barnes (Barnsie), the great saxophonist and clarinettist.

Born in 1932, the third child of four, John and his three sisters were a very close family. I believe they lost their postman father at an all too early age, leaving John the only man in the house and probably in a situation similar to my own, which ensured early maturity. Although no one played an instrument, the family all enjoyed music. From an early age, John was exposed to wartime songs, favourites of his two older sisters.

In his teens he learned to play the snare drum in the Boys' Brigade, and while rummaging around a junk shop, he discovered a clarinet and decided to have a go at that. John's first great love affair with jazz clarinet started with the New Orleans style of Johnnie Dodds, Jimmy Noone, and George Lewis, whose collective influences can still be heard in his playing. He co-founded what was probably the best known of the Manchester based bands, the Zenith Six. One of the great venues of the fifties and early sixties in the famous Cotton City was the Bodega; a large function room in a public house off Dean Street. This club regularly boasted visits from the more famous London based traditional styled bands, of which Mike Daniel's Delta Jazzmen was a typical and popular example.

The story goes that on one appearance at the club, Mike's regular clarinettist was indisposed. Spotting Barnsie in the audience, the bandleader approached the astonished clarinettist to ask if he had his instrument with him and if he would be prepared to fill the vacant chair on the stage for the duration of the performance. A dumbfounded, nervous, but nevertheless excited and thrilled young Barnes reticently agreed. From all reports he need not have worried, impressing the band and audience alike with his fluent playing.

A short time later, Mike's regular clarinettist left the band and John was contacted to see if he was interested in the position. It should at this stage be pointed out that good as they were the Delta Jazz Band never turned professional, Mike himself being the director of a small business. John's reply was a reluctant refusal, explaining that he had no job to go to in London and that he would be unable to live off semi-pro wages if he joined. Undaunted, Mike came up with the best possible answer; he would find a position in the firm's office for the young musician.

So John found himself in a strange office in the Capital, living in strange digs and with a strange bunch of musicians. I don't think the work in the office was too demanding as there seems to have been a lot of discussion about jazz music and the band, much to John's (who has always believed in fair pay for a fair day's work) discomfort. Mike had got his man and for the next year or two the clarinettist planted his roots in the metropolis in anticipation of the buds of a second-to-none reputation, and career in British jazz. He started lessons with the well-known teacher, Les Evans, who I believe forced him to unlearn the bad habits that had come with self-tuition.

In late 1960, or perhaps early 1961, Alan Elsdon left Terry Lightfoot's band to form his own. Among the personnel he invited to join was John Barnes, and it was under these circumstances that we met shortly after I had enrolled with the Clyde Valley Stompers, in May of the latter year. John had introduced his now famous sense of humour to his performances by then, and I recall thinking how entertaining Alan's outfit was on hearing them for the first time. Of course they were no different to the rest of us in their endeavour to gain fame, popularity, and ultimately financial reward, by including such classics as 'There's a Hole in my Bucket, Dear Lisa, Dear Lisa', featuring the falsetto talents of our hero. A good one that was! An article in the Melody Maker, reviewing the band, prophesied a silver-lined future. A couple of years later, with Alan's band descending the same downward path as most of the others, John left to join an equally struggling Alex Welsh.

Dear reader, before you bombard me with questions of John's National Service record, I will hereby enlighten you. He was conscripted into the heroic Royal Army Pay Corps for a brief and none-too-glorious twelve weeks, stationed at Devizes in Wiltshire. When asked to choose his preferences for possible postings, he chose Leeds (not too far from Manchester), and in his wife Pat's words, "Damn it, let's be adventurous", Hong Kong. Before any of this could take place, our boy was diagnosed to have a duodenal ulcer. Happily for all of us it was a wrong diagnosis, but not before the would-be soldier was returned post-haste to Civvy Street.

It was while with the Zenith Six, that John met his future partner the remarkable, long-suffering and patient, Pat. In her own words, this is how she describes the events that led to their marriage:

"I went to work in Manchester, where I heard the Zenith Six, having been introduced to the jazz music of Acker Bilk, when I was at college in Bristol. My flat mate and I became regular attendees at the Clarendon, a Zenith stronghold, and subsequently I went out with the bass player, Dick Lister, and she with John.

"In 1956, I headed for London. Friends from Bristol came to rescue me from my dreary suburban existence for a while. They took me to a party in Plaistow, where Acker and his band were living in a place over a factory. Buzzing about as one does at a party, I heard someone mention Johnny Barnes and discovered that he was the one and same I had met in Manchester. I did see him, but as he was flat out in bed, sleeping off the excesses of a good party, it was hardly an auspicious meeting. Months later, while seeking to escape my lonely suburb once more, I was mooching around the West End, when I ran into a girl I had known in Manchester. She was also looking for somewhere to stay. Finding somewhere in Chalk Farm, we moved in. Can you guess who had rented a room on the ground floor? Was this Kismet I sometimes ask myself?"

Roy Williams and John Barnes: the 'barefoot boys'

March 1937 was a good month for British Jazz, especially in Salford, now part of Greater Manchester; it saw the birth of multi-award winner, world-class trombonist, Roy Williams.

Born the second of three sons to Harold and Lillian, young Roy soon found himself on the move to 'safer' Farnworth, on the outskirts of Bolton, at the outbreak of the Second World War. As he grew up, he dabbled on the piano in a household in which music obviously played an important role. His engineering father could strum a lick or two on the then (and now again at the time of writing) fashionable ukulele and the boys were encouraged in any leanings toward music.

On leaving school, Roy was encouraged to follow in his father's footsteps and acquired an apprenticeship with the

Bolton Engineering firm of Entwistle and Gass. While working there, he was befriended by a one 'Bugs' Hodgkinson, who introduced him to the music called jazz. Although it seems Master Hodgkinson was a mite cloth-eared himself, Roy was deeply affected by this new music and he soon found himself looking for recordings, to further his education. He became friendly with a trumpet player called Bill Robinson, with whom he spent every Saturday morning in the local record shops searching for the latest gems. It was from these recordings that he heard Pete Daly's Chicagoans, and trombonist Warren Smith; his first great influence. Inspired and encouraged, Roy bought a trombone.

Together with Bill, and a few other young enthusiasts, the fledgling trombonist found a place to practice and play; in a freezing cold room above a pub, the York Hotel, every Saturday night. So cold and uncomfortable was the room, and so unhelpful the landlord, the young members of the newly named, Archimedes-inspired, Eureka Jazz Band, brought bags of coal and bundles of logs to kindle the fire in the arctic temperature of the room.

It wasn't long before the obvious talents of the young trombonist were spotted and his arrival circulated among the Manchester jazz fraternity, especially to the ears of an established band, the Southside Stompers. Mafiosi-like, Roy received an offer he couldn't refuse, and for the next nine months or so, learned to stomp with his new colleagues. This was short lived however, when he was asked once again at the end of a deferment, to accommodate his engineering apprenticeship and join another outfit; that of Her Majesty's Services in the shape of national conscription to the Armed Forces.

Most jazz musicians make useless soldiers as far as I can gather. I missed out on conscription by a couple of years, not reaching my eighteenth birthday until 1960. Len Hastings, Fred Hunt, and John Barnes, all without exception failed to make the grade demanded of the modern soldier, and Roy, although completing his full term, could hardly be described as military minded. In fact, I believe he was more of a nuisance than a help to his commanding officers, always being hauled over the coals for one misdemeanour or another, even ending up in the glasshouse on a couple of occasions. I believe he was posted to Belgium, and it was while he was there that he completed his military service in true 'jazzer's' style; playing the piano in the Sergeants' Mess. Roy had some formative piano lessons at some stage in his early years, but on his own admission, could never be described as a pianist.

At some point the position had been advertised, "Can any of you lot play the old 'Joanna' then?" Roy had straight away stuck up his hand. He got the 'skive' and served the rest of his time playing what must have been 'interesting' piano to (for the most part) tone-deaf ears of the British Army.

On his demobilisation, returning to Greater Manchester, Roy joined bassist Eric Batty's Jazz Aces, one of several good bands in that neck of the woods. I am told that there was a fair amount of rivalry (never, in my opinion a bad thing) among the Zenith Six, The Saints, and The Aces. One famous anecdote has passed on to jazz folklore from an evening when they were all involved.

A Jazz Extravaganza had been arranged to coincide with a tour of Britain by the great Sidney Bechet; I think he was playing with the Saints. At the end of the performance all the band leaders were invited on to the stage to add to 'When the Saints Go Marching in', by performing a solo chorus with the band. It was with great reluctance and much coercion that Eric, not known for his solo dexterity, stepped bass in hand to the microphone at the front of the stage when his turn came. I believe Roy was scarlet with embarrassment when the bassist sang his solo, emulating a bass, rather than show up his lack of musical prowess. I am told the unfortunate band leader never soloed again.

Roy by now had become too fine a trombonist to stay in Manchester, good as the bands there were, and soon agreed to travel south to London to join Mike Peters' Florida Jazzmen, featuring singer, Johnnie Silvo, of Playschool and folk music fame. The 'trad boom' was just around the corner with all its tatty hyperbole, cringe-worthy press releases, record company A&R men, and Mr ten-per-cent agents. Mike's agent, James

Tate, was typical. In his desire to sell his clients, he had a poster designed advertising the band's assets to include 'Hot Licks and Constant Raving'. As the boom took further hold on the undiscerning public, and in an effort not to be outdone by the likes of Kenny Ball and the others, our agent came up with what must be the dottiest suggestion for a tune ever offered to a jazz musician; "Six Green Jazz Musicians Playing on the Bandstand' - you must know it - *and if one green jazz musician should accidentally fall off and break his leg, there'd be five green jazz musicians playing on the bandstand.* I can just imagine Bix Beiderbecke doing justice to that one!

Roy was living around Twickenham, Strawberry Vale to be exact, with its proximity to Old Father Thames. He invested in a small boat and he moored her to some railings prior to departing on a short tour. On his return, setting off down to the river bank to make sure she was where he had left her (all boats are feminine are they not?), he was horrified to find the unfortunate craft lying at the bottom of the river. While he was away, the water level had risen quickly and substantially. While mooring, he had failed to notice a sharp spike above the boat under the railings. Water pressure and tidal movement had done their worst, holing the little vessel and scuppering her. I don't recall his enthusing, or even mentioning boats in all the years I've known him since then, his two passions being for model railways and cricket.

In 1960 he joined the recently formed Terry Lightfoot Band, which had the fine drummer, John Richardson, among its ranks. It was at the beginning of 1961 when I joined the Clydes that our paths first crossed. I had just been introduced to the famous Cottage Club, where jazzers' used to go for a legitimate late drink at none too cheap prices. (As we had entered the street where the notorious club was sited, we had narrowly avoided running over a shoe in the middle of the road.)

"I see Frank Parr's in!" exclaimed driver/trumpeter Malcolm Higgins, and sure enough, he was: shoeless and indeed 'legless'.

I had just obtained a mortgage to buy myself a drink and was feeding 'tanners' in the fruit machine when a red-faced, bouffant-style, red-headed, vaguely familiar stranger came across to me, pint in hand.

"I'm Roy Williams," he said, "mind if I join you?"

We seemed to get on right from the start; 'Steaming Jim and Raving Royston'. Of course our paths crossed frequently, what with jazz boat trips, all-nighters, and other extravaganzas, so that by the time he joined Alex's band, we were well acquainted. It's probably worth recalling an incident that happened on or about the second day after he joined the band, but first I must paint a little picture.

During his army days, Roy, like all red-blooded males, had attached a picture of an attractive nude pin-up to his locker door. In Roy's case the lady in question was Harrison Marks' famous 'Miss 44 Plus' Paula Page. Paula, or Brenda to give her real name, had been married to a car dealer, but had had a short affair with Alex, and had latched on to Fred Hunt, taking up residence with him and even adopting his surname. At rehearsal that afternoon, Fred had mentioned that his wife Brenda would be accompanying him to the 100 Club that evening. As the club at this time was still dry, we always met early for a taste in the Blue Posts pub. That night was no exception, and Roy was already at the bar when the couple arrived.

"Ah, Roy! This is Brenda," said Fred, introducing his attractive companion.

Roy's face was a mixture of delight, surprise and embarrassment as he shook hands with his hitherto two-dimensional heroine.

So now with the Manchester connection complete, the length and breadth of the country was represented within the band – a prile of Scots, a brace of Lancastrians, and a pair of Londoners – all speaking the universal language of jazz! There was never any disharmony between opposing geographical factions however. Good-natured 'send-ups' of the accents brought smiles and even giggles from the impersonated, who in return would mimic the mimicker's own natural dialect, often reducing the rest of the chaps to belly-clutching fits of laughter. The use of the Northern apostrophe was a fine example.

"Are you goin't watch match t'neet?" Fred might ask Roy.

"Not bleedin' loikely, moite!" was the reply.

Or:

"See yoo, Jummy! Urr yez gaun fur a drunk, the noo ye ken?" enquired JB to myself.

" Ee aye, bah goom, lad!" I might reply.

Len, who had a low threshold towards laughter, found all this extremely amusing and his infectious cackles would soon have us all literally on the floor. Barnsie especially was more often than not the instigator, getting all of us in turn to repeat some dialectic phrase such as: "Get yer dry slag frum Cloogsten's of Scoontherpe on t'Humberrr!"

He even at one stage recorded us on a portable cassette recorder to play the result back to us amid gales of laughter in some bar or hotel, when indulging in a 'latey', while he, beaming from ear to ear, would rub his hands and chest in frantic movements of delight. A tape recording of all this exists somewhere, probably in John's Isleworth emporium, but it must be extremely fragile by now and perhaps even unplayable. I hope not. I personally would love to hear the long departed voices of my colleagues again, not to mention Roy's timeless version of Stardust on the piano, under the pseudonym of Antonio Ronchordi, and Len's version of the Moon Landing.

Also in the emporium, acting as curator, but also suffering the ravages of time, is one time eighth member of the band, Angus Guidaye. Born, or rather acquired in a joke shop in Hull, Angus was adopted by John and soon became an inseparable friend to us all as one by one we succumbed to his encompassing personality. I think, for the uninitiated, I'd better explain: Guidaye is in fact a rubber mask. Picture if you will, a large cheery countenance made of slowly melting wax; thick lips grinning to reveal an incomplete set of irregular, discoloured, decaying teeth. High rosy-red cheekbones belied a slack jaw with its stubbly, unshaved chin, and an almost non-existent forehead was thatched with a shock of thick black hair. But here's the surprising thing; whosoever wore him immediately gave him a completely different appearance. Whether it had something to do with the shape of the wearer's face or his eyes, I have no idea. All I know is that Len Guidaye was entirely different from John Guidaye, etc. At some stage the wearer, I think Len, perched a flat cap on his head.

"He looks like a Scottish fitba' supporter!" exclaimed John, adopting his best Glaswegian accent, "Aye, guid, aye! C'moan ye bastarrrdd! Aye, guid, aye!"

And that's how he got his name. The Angus bit came later when John found, and doctored, an old passport for 'him' on a trip abroad. He went everywhere with us, travelling in John's baritone case and even from time to time appeared on the bandstand, playing one saxophone or another.

On one calamitous trip to Scotland in general, and my home village of Gifford in particular, he disappeared on a walk along one of Dr. Beeching's disused rail tracks. The entire contents of the Tweeddale Arms Public Bar, together with some local kids, sent out a search party for him. Luckily he was found, none the worse for his adventure, safe and well by the side of the pathway. He became known to musicians and friends in other outfits, and made friends with bar staff, hoteliers, restaurateurs, concert promoters and agents all over the place – even behind the Iron Curtain in the former East Germany. (He took on a definite Prussian appearance when worn by tour manager and radio presenter, Karl Heinz Drechsel.) I even heard him paged a couple of times in luxurious hotels and famous theatres. But the most remarkable, memorable, funniest recollection of Guidaye took place in the working men's' club at Newton Aycliffe, near Darlington in Northern England.

The band had been booked for a cabaret appearance at the club and had arrived early to set up. Relaxing at the bar, I was suddenly confronted by a beaming John Barnes.

"Come and see! Come and see! Guidaye's here!" He was shouting and pointing towards the lounge area. I half reluctantly left my bar stool and followed him. Looking in the direction of his gaze, I spotted a middle-aged chap wearing a cloth cap and a broad toothy smile. He was the spitting image of Angus Guidaye!

A sense of humour is paramount when seven guys are virtually living out of each other's pockets, day after day, night after night, week in, week out. Common interests are also important. We all loved our music of course, although some had leanings towards other *genres.d'art.* Most of us followed sport in one form or another. Reading and even board games such as Scrabble helped pass the time, and of course we all liked a drink.

John and Roy have several common interests such as model railways and classical music. Their common denominator however is, to this day, cricket. They are both members of the MCC and Lancashire CC, and proclaim their interest by wearing suitable neck ties when the occasion such as a test match arises. John has even organised a strolling band to play at Lord's whenever an important match is scheduled. He calls it John Barnes 'Out Swingers' if the weather is clement and 'In Swingers' if it rains.

In the seventies we played in an annual charity match at the Credit Lyonnaise Bank's sports ground at Chingford, North London, against a Jimmy Greaves Eleven – a team picked from a combination of West Ham United and Tottenham Hotspur footballers. To bring a little balance to the affair, we were allowed to enlist the help of one professional cricketer, a very good Lancashire League wicket keeper and good friend of the band in general (and Roy in particular), Bolton schoolmaster and jazz buff, Peter Stafford, and another friend and fine batsman, Nick Morgan. Nick's father, a gentleman and lover of our music, and the person, I believe, responsible for John and Roy gaining membership of the MCC, stood as umpire. Strangely enough, we turned to the Yorkshire CC for first Don

Wilson, the fine spin bowler and the following year, Phillip Sharpe, the great slip fielder. It's not as strange as it sounds! The guys had befriended Don through his love of jazz and their passion for cricket, and in his testimonial year, he booked the band for his ball. We found the team to consist of a great bunch of fellows. Over the course of the next few years we played for several of their functions and became firm friends with the likes of Barry Leadbetter, Jack Hampshire, Phil Sharpe, and the late David Bairstow. They in turn attended jazz clubs and concerts when we were performing, and were even known to turn up at the occasional party at Barnsie's house when they were playing at Lord's.

With the exception of Geoffrey Boycott, whom I found to be distant and aloof, we enjoyed their company immensely. I still see Jack Hampshire at Lords when I play banjo in John's band, and he is still 'hail fellow, well met!' to both of us with always a fond recollection of the days gone by. It was with great sadness that I read of the tragic death of David Bairstow. He was such a happy-go-lucky sort of a chap when in our company.

The charity matches were great fun although the cricketing standard of the band was nothing to write home about, apart from the two professionals. I shared a three-ball stand for the sixth wicket with Phil Sharpe, and unfortunately the scorebook reads: four, dot, out clean bowled – Phil Beale. But we won the match the first year, thanks to D Wilson, and accepted an honorary draw in the second. There was no competition at the bar afterwards, however.

The footballers, with the exception of their non-playing captain 'Greavsie', who was still quaffing a tot or six, were mostly abstainers, or at best, light drinkers. The chaps on the other hand were seasoned campaigners in the noble Bacchanalian recreational cause. No contest!

Musically both Roy and John had followed similar paths. From being 'mouldy figs' they had gradually veered towards Dixieland and Mainstream through the influences of Jelly Roll Morton, Louis' Hot Fives and Sevens, Eddie Condon, and their likes. But all roads lead to Rome and true to this, they found their direction led to the same jazz *colossi*; Bob Brookmeyer and Gerry Mulligan, and their distinctive outlook on jazz.

While the rhythm section was setting up their instruments one day, John was noodling a version of 'Sweet Georgia Brown" he had been listening to, on his baritone. Roy, recognising the piece, immediately joined in. Bubbling with enthusiasm, Roy suggested another, Bike Up the Strand, based on George Gershwin's, 'Strike up the Band'. That sounded great too!

"Do you know, "Open Country'?" he asked.

"I think so!" replied John, having a stab at the Brookmeyer composition. Working out the chords, Ron Mathewson and I joined in.

"Let's do it tonight," said John, "we'll be a small band within a small band!"

It was an immediate success. Sometimes they played it as a quartet, giving me a number off and changing the sound of the band completely. 'Open Country' led to versions of both 'Crazy' and 'Fascinatin' Rhythm', all with equal success. But perhaps the most memorable sound Roy and John added to the band was their vocal harmonising with Alex. Roy, of course, sang on his featured version of Tangerine, and John on a couple of songs such as 'Doctor Jazz', and 'You're Drivin' me Crazy', but it was I believe at an after-hours party at the Brecon Hotel in Rotherham, that the possibilities presented themselves. Len, naturally, had started the whole thing off with his 'cod' German piece 'Auf wiedersehn', to be joined by Alex, trousers rolled to the knee, standing on chairs for, 'You Are my Hearts Delight'. After Fred had played a couple of Ivor Novello 'evergreens', and I had sewn myself into a ball with an invisible needle and thread, Roy sat down at the piano. Finishing 'Stardust', to rapturous applause and hearty laughter, he began to sing and accompany himself on an old ditty called 'In Barefoot Days'.

"I know that one," exclaimed John, "it's an old Lancashire folk song!"

Moving to the side of the 'Joanna', he took up the harmony. Hand movements and gestures in the old vaudeville style followed, and the whole number came to climactic finale with both of them on their feet holding a long chord and performing a sort of shuffling tap dance, reminiscent of Wilson, Kepple and Betty. It was hilarious! Although it was not used on the stage at the time, it became an absolute must at parties and after-performance drink-ups. Whether or not it was a Lancastrian folk song, or a Cockney one as Jack Peacock insists, it will forever be for me associated with the Barefoot Boys, as they became known. My life has certainly been made richer by their wonderful version of the old ditty. Among the most popular were such vocal extravaganzas as 'Dapper Dan', 'Happy Feet', 'When you wore a Tulip', 'Toot Toot, Tootsie', 'Wait 'til the Sun Shines, Nellie', and later a splendid version of a seventies pop song, 'Tie a Yellow Ribbon Round the Old Oak Tree', arranged by vibraphonist, Roger Nobes.

In my opinion, the Barefoot Boys were the greatest thing to ever happen to the Alex Welsh Band. They were largely responsible for expanding the already broad versatility for which the band had become famous, and no matter what style of music they were performing, kept to an amazingly high musical standard, and gave one hundred percent effort in doing so.

CHAPTER SIX

I JUST BLEW IN FROM THE WINDY CITY

The storm damage caused by Whirlwind Henry had hardly been repaired when England was visited by two completely contrasting winds blowing from the same direction: Chicago. First came a gentle zephyr in the form of Eddie Condon's side man, Charles Ellsworth 'Pee Wee' Russell. Although he was not every clarinettist's cup of tea, the late Mr Russell had long been one of my heroes, and I awaited his arrival with anticipation and excitement.

Tales of Pee Wee's drinking and frailty had been drifting across the Atlantic for years so that when I laid eyes on him for the first time, I was surprised by his healthy appearance. He was taller than I expected, immaculately dressed, and had a twinkle in his eye, which belied the natural frown that always seemed to adorn his countenance. Accompanying him was his attractive and ever watchful wife, Mary. When asked if he would care for a drink he simply requested a glass of milk. Later we discovered that out of sight of his caring spouse, he took to slipping a little brandy in the glass – undetectable, but beneficial and probably the source of the aforementioned twinkle.

At rehearsal we noticed how quietly he played, but thought he was holding back, saving himself for the evening performance. How wrong can one be? He always played like that. None of the raucous, note-holding, vibrato-filled diarrhoea associated with the wailing, screeching drivel offered by the typical 'liquorice stick' owner of the recent trad boom. His soft woody tone and economic, well-chosen notes, especially in the ensemble passages, was a lesson for all of them to learn. Occasionally he did blow out, soaring in the higher register in the familiar jerky way, so familiar with the Condon Gang. Sometimes in fact, the band must have sounded highly reminiscent of that sound, especially with John Barnes on baritone sax.

The high spot of the performance was undoubtedly his solo with just the rhythm section, an original composition called 'Pee Wee's Blues'. Though just a blues, the structure of the piece was dramatically, radically different, inasmuch as the composer had used a semi-tone drop in the chord structure of the first four bars, and a whole tone scale towards the end. At a medium-slow tempo the soloist would state the melody softly and warmly, before building to a climax in the penultimate chorus. Returning to the haunting melody, Pee Wee would gradually decrease the volume in a dynamic *diminuendo,* in which all that could be heard was the gentle rattle of the keys beneath his fingers. I remember tears in John's eyes and the hairs prickling on the nape of my neck as the audience responded with rapturous applause. As he turned to acknowledge the rhythm section, a half smile played on his lips and his right eye formed a mischievous wink humorously contorting the craggy, clownish features. I'll never forget it.

Of course, there are thousands of anecdotes about the Eddie Condon Band, and Pee Wee features in many of them. Other (perhaps more illustrious) authors and collectors of such tales will have catalogued the more important ones and we are all grateful to them for their efforts. Nevertheless, as this is a recollection of my personal memories, I would like to pass on one cracker, as I recall it.

The Condon Band, to help pass long sessions at the club, would often play ballad medleys, where each soloist would play a favourite song in turn, informing the pianist of his selection in the course of the previous soloist's offering. One evening, Pee Wee, not noted for his overuse of words anyway, possibly through a combination of booze and nerves, either couldn't remember the title of his selection, or simply couldn't get it out. He stood on the stage, making snake-like movements with his right arm, followed by both arms flapping by his sides. Pianist, Gene Schroeder, without hesitation went straight into Can't Help Loving that Man of Mine. Pee Wee was conveying in mime, fish gotta swim, birds gotta fly.

As the tour progressed, Charles Elsworth became more relaxed and began to talk more freely, even telling stories of the early Condon days. To emphasise punch-lines or important passages, he would interpolate the sentence with a loud utterance of the word "Bang!" I recall the surprise the first time we heard him say it but, naturally, of course, long after he was back in the States, the chaps were 'banging' like good-'uns. Unfortunately, he only came on one short tour. We met him briefly again when he appeared with us at the Newport Jazz Festival shortly before his all-too-early demise. I listen to his music frequently and never fail to get a lump in my throat when I hear the soulful Pee Wee's Blues.

Sketch by Jimmy Thompson

The zephyr slowly died away, to be replaced by a force nine gale, in the shape of William 'Wild Bill' Davison. Of course, his reputation had forewarned us and some of the guys had actually met him when he visited these shores with Eddie Condon in the fifties and more recently on his aforementioned tour with Freddie Randall but, somehow, here he was, even larger in life than we had imagined. Yes, here he was, gum-chewing, loud-mouthed, hard-drinking, flirtatious, extrovert 'Wild William', in the flesh and raring to go.

He arrived at the Manchester Sports Guild for the customary rehearsal, having travelled north with several members of the band. They looked shell-shocked. Soon enough I would find out why. The man was a human dynamo.

"Ain't they got any booze in this M-F place?" were nearly enough the first words he uttered. Alex usually had a little 'wet' to help him on his travels, but that had been well and truly seen off on the journey, even though there had been a couple of pub stops as well. The proprietor, Jenks, duly obliged and we got down to business.

At this stage the band was still playing in a predominantly Chicago Dixieland style so, when Bill put the cornet to his mouth (curiously, he had adopted a slightly off-centre embouchure, which gave a little tilt to his head), it was as if he had been playing with the band all his life. As he blew, I noticed that he removed the horn from his mouth after every phrase, using the interim moment to masticate the omnipresent gum several times before restoring it to one cheek in preparation for tonguing the next phrase. I often wondered what would happen if it got stuck in his mouthpiece, but it never happened. I caught sight of Alex and Roy Crimmins; they had grins wide enough to split their faces in two. Fred also, and Lennie! After the run-through, which incidentally bore no resemblance to the performance that evening, we walked back to the hotel on a cushion of air and alcohol, leaving just enough time for a short nap and a bath before kick-off.

I don't have to tell you how wonderful playing with Bill was - you can hear for yourselves. One of the MSG performances was recorded for issue in America, but the good news is that 'Blowin' Wild' is now available as a Jazzology CD in this country. Perhaps you've already purchased it – if not, treat yourself!

Everywhere we played, it was the same story. Not only did we have the best Dixieland cornet player in Britain leading the band, we also had his mentor. When they were both on the stand at the same time the music was electric, as both men fed off each other. Of course, it wasn't just his playing that made Bill; I believe that basically he was quite nervous and shy, and used a form of brashness to overcome this. Perhaps you remember his non-stop chat on the stand, but I'll bet you never heard what he was saying. Perhaps that is just as well. I'll tell you one of his regular little niceties, though: if, while playing, he spotted an attractive female jiving in front of the band, he would in a none-too-quiet voice sing, "Though she dresses so divine, her ass hole smells the same as mine." Or, "Did you get a look at the boobies on that M-F?" he would utter with one had cupping his mouth, but loudly enough for all on the stand to hear.

Each day brought another adventure and a couple come to mind readily. In all, Bill made dozens of visits to these shores. At one time he had even taken up residence in Denmark, resulting in his easy availability to Europe in general, and as my memory refuses to isolate individual incidents to any particular tour, please forgive me for any chronological errors in my ramblings.

I do remember my first tale happening in a hotel where we were playing and staying, in Stourbridge, Worcestershire. After the usual storming concert, we congregated at the bar for a 'latey', and as usual it was well into the morning before we hit the sack. I had only been in my room for about five minutes, when I heard Bill noisily letting himself into his quarters, which were adjacent to mine. Suddenly there came a loud thud through the wall and I was on my feet in an instant. On reaching his room, I noticed the door ajar. I wasn't quite prepared for the sight that met my eyes, though, as I stepped into the room. On the floor, on his back with his knees up round his ears, was our hero. He was frantically pulling at something by his feet.

"For Chrissake, help me!" he cried, bursting into peals of laughter.

Then I spotted his predicament. He had tried to remove his trousers without slipping his braces from his shoulders, and as a result his feet were trapped at the waistband. It only took a minute to extricate him from his predicament and he staggered to his feet, murmuring his thanks. Now, clad in blazer, collar and tie, socks and underpants, my hero picked up a duffel bag and with the words, "Here, I got something for you," he emptied the contents over the bed. Among several items of cutlery (souvenirs), dozens of packets of gum, and a few other personal items, he found a multi-opener – you know the kind that can open anything worth opening. Handing it to me, he uttered the words, "Take this, it'll help you through life."

On a later tour, we had occasion to go into the studio to cut another album with Bill, as part of a series of important recordings produced by Terry Brown on the Fontana label. Because we had already appeared somewhere else that evening, the session was fixed to start at about midnight. This policy was often adopted for recording, the theory being that the musicians would be nice and relaxed and therefore less nervous. This was a good idea, provided the artists hadn't spent too much time with 'John Barleycorn' during the earlier part of the evening. On this occasion, we were all still high from the early performance, as well as slightly weary and therefore relaxed, and the resulting album proved quite rewarding. The only reserve I would personally make is that most of the material on the album was slightly over-arranged and therefore didn't have the spark so obvious on 'Blowin' Wild'. Nevertheless, it was an enjoyable session, made all the more memorable by what took place at the end of the night, or rather in the wee small hours of the morning.

At one point during the session, Herr Hastings had produced the famous German tin helmet he sported during his act. It had also transpired during one of the tours, that Wild Bill was a collector of, among other things, German war memorabilia. He had had his eye on this helmet for some time. Fortunately, Len had recently acquired another so, albeit a little reluctantly, he presented the trophy to 'Kaiser Bill'. It never left his head for the rest of the recording session, but the best was still to come. My last sight of Bill that morning was of him still wearing the helmet whilst hailing a black London cab. Maybe London had been invaded after all!

Wild William and Alex showing off their 'King' cornets

As the years went by, Wild Bill visited Britain many times, accompanied usually by his lovely wife, Annie. Although a little more subdued and on his best behaviour most of the time under her caring, watchful eye, he always produced exciting, inspiring music. We all became very good friends, and to me, it was a delight to be referred to as 'our Scottish grandson'.

It was heartbreaking to read his obituary by that fine writer, Steve Voce, one morning in The Independent newspaper. I believed that, like his music, Wild William would live forever.

To commemorate his birthday a year after his passing, Annie chartered a little aeroplane to tow a banner across the Santa Barbara skyline.

"WE LOVE YOU WILD BILL!" it read.

Indeed, we do!

CHAPTER SEVEN

THE SWINGING TRAMP

I first came across extrovert drummer, Lennie Hastings, backstage in the Corn Exchange dance hall in Haddington, East Lothian, around 1958. Dressed in a Country and Western outfit, he was deep in conversation with the great guitarist, Denny Wright and a bunch of enthusiastic Skiffle-mad kids (yours truly included), and talking in a very bad Americanised Cockney accent. Lennie was the drummer with the Blue Grass Boys, an English group backing Tennessee-born Johnnie Duncan, and was probably enjoying the most financially secure part of his all-too-short life. It was probably also the most wasteful, as he spent as quickly as he earned, in an effort to get over a recently broken marriage.

'Herr' Lennie Hastings

Leonard was born in Carshalton, Surrey. His father, George, was a bus conductor, who had leanings toward the stage, in particular Music Hall and Vaudeville (he once performed Burlington Bertie for me when he was well into his seventies and struggling for breath due to emphysema). As a youth in war torn London, directly under the flight paths of the airborne invasion by Goering's Luftwaffe, Len had taken a job as a bread delivery boy in the area around Rose Hill, in the district of Morden.

On one memorable day, he was pushing his handcart towards the top of the hill when he heard the unmistakable sound of a Doodle-bug – a German flying bomb – approaching. Suddenly the bomb's planned fuel supply expired and the engine cut out. Knowing that the propelled weapon's descent was imminent, our hero dived under his cart, covering his eyes with his fingertips and sticking his thumbs in his ears, in a vain attempt to protect himself. After what seemed an age he heard the sound of a muffled explosion in the distance and he opened his eyes to see his cart at the bottom of the hill and a trail of bread down the road.

At about the same time, he was a member of a local jazz appreciation society, which met weekly to discuss the latest hot news and listen to the latest available 78's. There was often a blind fold test, a competition among the members to spot and identify musicians on record. On one occasion, the object of the test was a well-known clarinettist. Among the participants was a young member who had a speech impediment in the form of a stammer. His knowledge of jazz and its musicians was paramount.

"Meh...Meh...Meh....Meh...." The unfortunate fellow struggled to answer, whereupon the rest of the fans, much to the chagrin of the poor man, shouted simultaneously: "Mezz Mezzrow!"

Already playing drums, Lennie had joined a semi-professional band called the Rug Cutters, led by a fine pianist by the name of Mike Brian, and which on occasion had boasted the presence of several promising young jazzers including

Gerry Salisbury, and Victor Feldman. An adolescent George Shearing was also making his mark. With this obviously great introduction to jazz, it wasn't long before the young drummer decided to turn professional. He was fifteen years old.

There was nothing unusual in the tenderness of his years, remembering that school leaving age was about fourteen or even earlier then, but it should come as a surprise to you, as it did to me, when I tell you the band he joined was that of Myra Morris and her Juvenile Rhythm Queens. I believe Len's education took a step forward as a result of that adventure!

Soon military service beckoned and Private Hastings found himself in the Army. He was a wily codger though, and found ways (usually hat-related), of wangling out of drill parades and exercises with one trumped-up excuse or another. While resting in his billet one day an amusing event occurred.

Among the camp personnel was a retired Regimental Sergeant Major, acting as a gardener. So fearful and unhappy was this man about the prospect of life outside the Army, that he had volunteered his services to horticulture tasks to enable him to keep contact with the only lifestyle he had known. Lying on his bed one summer day, no doubt nursing a severe headache from the wearing of his beret, Len heard the raised voice of the gardener drifting through his open window.

"Call yourself a cabbage?" the voice asked.

Stealthily looking out of the window, Len spotted the ex-sergeant looking at a small green object in his large red hand.

"Call yourself a cabbage?" he repeated, and doing an immaculate about-turn, marched across the plot. "I'll show you a cabbage!"

Kneeling down, he presented the offending vegetable to a much larger version, shouting, "That's a cabbage!"

"Call yourself a cabbage?" was adopted and used by the AW band whenever anything less than presentable was evident. Possibly because of his unwillingness to be a normal soldier, but more likely because of his musical talents, Lennie found himself posted to 'Stars in Battledress', a sort of ENSA, sharing a billet with the late Benny Hill. I believe they were both influential in each other's careers, Len at least showing the same zany sense of humour in later years with the AW band.

The next time his name cropped up, Len had joined the very fine Freddie Randall band, and from this period in his life came many oft-repeated anecdotes, one of which will suffice here.

To all intents and purposes, and probably for economic reasons, the Randall bus was like a travelling hotel. There were makeshift beds on board and even a Primus stove to cook and heat food. Journeys in those days, let us not forget, were lengthy affairs and time was of great importance. Freddie's driver was also the trombonist, Norman Cave. On one sadly memorable occasion while touring Scotland, he failed to negotiate a bend on a bridge, culminating in a broken arm and a hospital bed for himself, as well as an impromptu serving of hot rabbit stew for the band, which tenor saxophonist, Betty Smith, was cooking at the time. That evening, the group of travel-weary slightly bruised musicians, took to the stage at the Kirkcaldy Ice Rink, trombone-less. There is intensity in the nature of the Scot, in my experience, to always want things to be right. On this occasion, two diehard Jocks approached Freddie to ascertain the whereabouts of the missing musician. Freddie informed them of the accident, and with little concern for the welfare of Norman, or indeed the rest of the band, one turned to the other and in broad local tones said, "Oh crivens! Did ye hearrrrr that, Harrrrry? Nae trumboan! Nae tumboan!"

Fortunately, Norman made a full recovery.

In 1954, several disgruntled members of Freddie's band, namely Lennie, Archie Semple, Fred Hunt, and Roy Crimmins, approached Alex (who was supplementing the Mick Mulligan Band at that time) to take the trumpet chair in a breakaway band they had the idea of forming, and Alex agreed to join. However, when it came to the crunch, nobody seemed to want to lead the band and a vote was cast for either Alex or Roy Crimmins to determine a leader. Fate decided that Alex drew, in his words, the short straw between himself and Roy. All this proved a sickening blow to Freddie Randall and he never forgave Alex, despite the latter being blameless of any conspiracy to start a new band. All Alex said he ever wanted to do was play Jazz Band Ball.

It was in this new band that the love-hate relationship between Alex and Lennie was spawned. Although history has proved that musically, they could not live without each other, they bickered constantly. After a few months, the inevitable happened. It was New Year's Eve and the band, their wives, girlfriends, and pals had congregated at Alex's flat to see in the New Year. The party lasted well into the wee small hours, by which time it was too late for Len to get transport home and he probably couldn't afford it, anyway. Alex agreed he could stay until morning, and somehow or other they ended up in the same double bed. At this juncture it should be mentioned (if not obvious to those who have known them both over the years), that there was no question of anything untoward happening, both being confirmed heterosexuals and raving womanisers. Alex awoke first and, as he told me later, lay in bed thinking about the "snoring heap next to me," and getting more and more angry about all the trouble the drummer had caused over the previous few months. The moment Len awoke, Alex blurted out, "Happy New Year, and by the way, you're fired!" It was soon after that that Lenny joined Johnny Duncan's Blue Grass Boys.

Duncan was a genuine American. Born in the Blue Grass Mountains of Virginia, he was a small man with a high tenor voice, almost in the *falsetto* range. As a direct result of the interest in Skiffle music, created by Ken Colyer, Chris Barber, and most of all, Lonnie Donegan, several American stars famous in the country/blues idiom were invited to visit this country. Duncan had settled here, having married during his stint as a GI. He formed a group consisting of the aforementioned British musicians (Lennie and Denny Wright), and Canadian bassist, Jack Fallon, and had a series of colossal hits.

Among those visitors gracing our concert halls at that time were Big Bill Broonzy, Sister Rosetta Tharpe, and Sonny Terry/Brownie McGhee, who worked as a duo. Sonny was sightless and almost totally dependent on Brownie. At one concert they were due to appear on stage immediately after Duncan's Blue Grass Boys.

Standing in the wings, on hearing Johnny's high-pitched vocals, a confused Sonny was heard to ask, "Hey, Brownie! Who's dat gal singer out dere wid dat Johnny Duncain?"

However, it wasn't long before a revival in the public's interest in jazz and a decline in Skiffle's popularity led to Lennie's re-joining The Alex Welsh Band. (In the interim years, Alex had found a fine drummer in John Richardson, who had moved on to the Terry Lightfoot Band.) By the time our paths crossed again, I was with the Clydes, and Lennie had re-joined Alex. The only concessions Alex had made to being accepted on the trad scene were to add a banjo player, Tony Pitt, who doubled fine guitar. Alex had recorded two or three singles aimed at the popular end of the market: Cole Porter's pretty song, 'Rosalie'; a boring (in my opinion) clarinet feature, obviously aimed at the 'Petite Fleur' market, written by Norrie Paramor, and saved from extinction by Archie Semple, called, 'Tansy"; and a double-A-sided single of 'Auf Wiedersehen, My

Dear', and 'Ein, Zwei Solfe', with vocals by 'Herr Lennie Hastings mit Alexbaum Welshbach und Sein Kapelle'. Although the marketing was, in my opinion, stupid and a little bit amateurish, the contents were fun and the record enjoyed some success.

Len's prowess as a drummer is well documented by the many recordings he is featured on, but his harmless eccentricity is perhaps less publicised. He had three main heroes: Winston Churchill, Adolf Hitler, and the famous Austrian operetta tenor, Richard Tauber. Churchill he held in utmost respect, while Hitler and Tauber, although respectful of their obvious talents of oration and singing, he considered as almost comical caricatures. He found something incredibly humorous in the pantomime-like presentation in their modus operandi. He parodied both of them on stage, screwing a monocle into his left eye and adopting a Hitler-like stance to 'cod' his way through a Lehar classic in a German language only he understood, which included such classic Teutonic phrases as 'ze fisch und chips'.

Later he took to wearing an authentic German tin helmet given to him by some admirer, and which had been added to his private collection of wartime memorabilia that accompanied him everywhere in a small brown Globetrotter suitcase. He had collected armbands, badges, iron crosses, various shirts, hats, and jackets, and other odds and sorts. To these he added old toupees, dyed black and combed to one side, and a small collection of black combs. In the privacy of his home or hotel room, he would dress himself as his misguided hero.

By way of sponsorship by the Swiss COOP, and organised by the late Rene Hahn, Alex's band had toured Switzerland several times in the late 1950's and early sixties. The tour consisted mainly of concerts, often in the same hotel as the band accommodation. The story of a famous event that took place on one such occasion has been well narrated, but I would like to silence any Chinese whispers and relate what really happened.

A party among the band, their wives, friends, and invited fans, had broken out in a room on the top floor of such a hotel. As the sound from the party swelled in volume, there had been some complaints made by other guests to the night porter. The porter, doing his duty, had telephoned the party room on several occasions to convey the complaints. Lennie, by this time, had adopted his full 'Fuhrer' persona, including wig, moustache, armbands et al, and was well into the part. The last call from the concierge had threatened police action so it was decided that Herr Hitler should take the situation in hand. Entering the lift, he descended to the ground floor. As the door opened he stepped forward, raised his right arm in the Nazi salute and shouted, "Zieg Heil!"

As the doors closed on the retreating drummer, the concierge picked up the telephone. "Police? There are some

Britishers having a loud party in one of the rooms and what's more they have Adolf Hitler with them!"

The police never arrived.

It was around this time that the famous 'Oolyah, oolyah' cry was born but, contrary to general belief, it was first uttered by bassist Chris Staunton. It happened in a venue I was to visit many years later, but had established itself in the band's history for several reasons including the former. This was the Dusseldorf New Orleans Jazz Club. The club room supported a tiny bandstand, at the back of which a door led down some stairs to the cellar cloakrooms and toilets. This door was situated just at the position on the stage adopted by the bassist. Chris was a quiet, intelligent man of few words, but several expressive sounds and grunts. Like most of the band, he enjoyed a pint or two. German hospitality to musicians is renowned and here was no exception.

One evening, probably feeling tired from the booze and the long hours expected from bands, Chris was leaning on this door while playing. Suddenly the door sprang open and the bass and player tumbled down the stairs. As he fell he emitted a loud "Oooorrllyyaahhh!" before dusting himself down and re-ascending the stairs; unhurt, he carried on playing. At the end of the number, Len incorporated his version of the yell in his four bar drum break, much to the delight of the audience who had witnessed the entire event. During the course of the rest of the performance, and indeed from that time on, "Oolyah" became a jealously guarded part of his repertoire, even to the extent of his consideration of patenting it to prevent other drummers mimicking him. Years later, as a result of its popularity, the 'word' became part of the name for an organisation running several jazz venues, known as the 'Oolyah, Oolyah, Club'.

Several years later, we were back in Dusseldorf for the Rheinland Fasching Festival. Hotels and restaurants all around were packed and a carnival air pervaded the city. Our hotel, the Vossen, sat to one side of a busy market square, full of candy stalls, side shows, and the like. Marching up and down and in and out the stalls, was a typical German band, the sound of which drew me to my balcony window. Looking down on the square I spotted John and Roy doubled up with laughter. Thinking I shouldn't miss out on whatever was the source of their merriment, I joined them. Still in stitches they pointed to the first floor of our hotel. There on his balcony, completely suitably attired, was Herr Hastings, arm raised in mock salute, marching in time to the band up and down the length of his balcony and occasionally turning to face the square as if addressing a Nuremburg rally.

During the fifteen years or so I shared my life with Len, I got to learn of his ideals, idols, foibles, and fancies, and indeed the complexity of his varied lifestyle in general. Twice married and the father of six handsome children, born in and out of wedlock, he was happily settled in Twickenham with his second wife, Janet and daughter, Jane, when I joined the band. Although casually dressed almost to the point of scruffy in his day-to-day attire, Lennie scrubbed up well, and with the help of a toupee or 'Irish' as he referred to it, and Leichner No.5 actors' make-up, he became quite the reverse on stage. At least at the beginning of the evening this was the case. As the G&T's and bitter ale descended the drummer's gullet, things became a little more casual. The jacket was first off, quickly followed by the tie, shirt sleeves rolled up next, and finally the shirt itself opened to the waist displaying a tee shirt and grey hairs on the partly revealed chest. Finally, as perspiration rolled down from his brow, his specs would find their way into a pocket, leaving him with a slightly bewildered look as he struggled to focus. His final prosthetic was a small denture with a couple of teeth attached, which he wore to fill a gap in his upper palate. This he removed to eat, slipping the object into his trouser hip-pocket. Of course, this was obviously often left un-replaced, to later remind its owner of its existence in the most obvious manner.

"Blimey! I've been bitten in the arse again!" was often his way of finding out, and reaching into his pocket for the offending article it would be retrieved and re-inserted into his mouth, un-rinsed.

In the Peter Wyngarde-inspired early seventies, Len decided to have a suit made to be with the fashion. We waited with excited anticipation and when the great unveiling came, were pleasantly surprised at the result. The suit was of a brownish grey material with large lapels on the fitted jacket and flared trousers. Very smart, we all agreed. But within a month, the Post Office decided to re-attire its staff, and overnight the drummer became a postman. Same style. Same colour. There's a spy in the camp!

He introduced me to horse racing for which I really to this day have no liking, but it was his passion. I think I ought to clarify this a little. It was betting that was his passion, and while at the races he would spend his time between perusing the latest odds, gin and tonics, and jellied eels. These two gastronomic delights were handled by him in a totally opposite manner. The drink would come first of course, but it was consumed in a form of self-torture. Filling a tall glass with ice cubes and a slice of lemon, he would trickle the gin over them and lastly pour in the tonic water. Then he waited...and waited...and finally when the outside of the glass was frosted with condensation, with a great gasp of anticipatory delight he would drain the glass in one swallow, rubbing his chest gleefully while he emitted more sounds of joyful satisfaction. The eels were approached in a different way. There would be the same masochistic pleasure gained by refraining to buy them until he could wait no longer, but the moment the tub was in his hands it seemed to empty by magic. A good burp was the signal of his complete enjoyment.

As for the actual racing, as I said, he was only interested in form, but never seemed to read it to his advantage as he always seemed to lose. He was a coincidence better; one day he bet on horses with a proper name, or just initials, and the next it could be a colour in their titles. It was often the jockey's fault when they lost: "That bleedin' Piggott couldn't ride a rockin' 'orse!" or, "F...ing Breasley!" and the such like, as he watched his hard earned cash disappear.

On the other hand, as is often the case of someone knowing nothing about the subject, I often won by sheer luck. On such occasions I made sure that he didn't want for a drink or a bite to eat by offering him a small part of my winnings as a tide over till he got paid again. On these occasions I was often the loser, but what the hell, I was single and therefore better off and I enjoyed his company so much it was worth every penny.

His masochistic tendencies had come to the fore in his adolescence when he had contrived some kind of self-punishment by the use of a bamboo cane and a door jamb.

"What you doing up there?" his mother would call up the stairs, perhaps better off for never finding out. Later he told us he used to visit a certain type of lady with the exotic name of Anita Wyplash, when his desires for correction got the better of him. It takes all sorts to make the world a better place, and as for Len, a kinder, more well-mannered gentleman to the ladies never drew breath. Although perhaps a little uncouth in his own behaviour, he detested anyone else's bodily functions, like farting, belching, spitting, or sneezing. I remember once at a late night drink somewhere, a female admirer was sitting on

Len's hand in his lap when she suddenly, involuntarily, passed wind. He expelled her from her position like a ball from a cannon, with a look of horror and disgust on his face. That was the end of that romance!

As I said earlier, Len and I travelled together with the equipment in his little van. There was nothing we liked better than to set off early, get the journey out of the way, and book into the hotel in time for a lunchtime pint, leaving the afternoon free to follow our own individual pursuits and pastimes. I favoured a few holes of golf, or if it was a Saturday in Manchester and United were at home, then I went to the match. Len went to the betting shop to place a few losers, and then retired for a couple of hours in the privacy of his room.

One particular Saturday afternoon in Manchester, through fatigue from travelling and lunch, Len had decided on a little lie down before the evening gig. The hotel we used, because of its proximity to the Sports Guild, was invariably the Mitre, with our chosen watering hole, the Shambles, also close by. On the other side of the hotel stood the impressive towering edifice of Manchester Cathedral. The two contrasting buildings were barely separated from each other by a footpath.

This particular afternoon (or perhaps every Saturday afternoon), the cathedral's campanologists had decided that some practice was in order, and promptly around three pm, had entered into it with gusto. As the sounds drifted into the bedrooms of the somnolent 'musos', the first sounds of disgruntlement were heard from the drummer's room.

"Belt up!"

After a few more utterances there came the sound of a door slamming and footsteps passing along the corridor. Looking out of the window on to the concourse, I spotted Len, still wearing pyjamas but with a leather jacket over his shoulders and a flat cap on his wig-less head, approaching the wrought iron gate that opened on to the cathedral grounds. Walking up to the door, which he found to be locked, he started pounding on it with clenched fists.

"Belt uuuupppp! Fucking beeeelltttt uuuppp! F...uck off!

Getting no reply from the now fully flowing bell ringers, the red faced crestfallen percussionist turned on his heel and headed back to his room, to rescue what part of the afternoon was left to him, while six other chaps chortled quietly from theirs.

I miss Len to this day. I was in Nice, in July 1978, when I heard of his death and it took from me all the pleasures of the festival with all its famous guests. It came as little surprise, of course, as for a time he had been convalescing from a massive stroke and we were told he could suffer another at any time. I purposely didn't visit because I didn't want to see him handicapped as he was, and contented myself by sending messages to him through others, who in return, gave me progress reports on his condition. John Barnes was one of the most frequent, being the sort of chap he is, and because of the close proximity of his home. He described a typical visit to me that told of the drummer's frustrations, caused by his inability to pronounce words. Pointing angrily with his finger he would utter, "Doodee deedee doodee deedee dooo!" ending as frustration mounted, "doodee fucking doo!"

As a footnote to this chapter on one of the most charismatic characters I have ever met, I am going to break my own rules a little by mentioning once more his offspring. As I have intimated, there were six, of whom I have little knowledge, with the exception of his two daughters by his second wife Janet, Jane and Claire, whose acquaintances I have recently renewed and who were around for all the time I knew him. I never met his first child, Julie, or any of his sons, but will end on a little information I gleaned from John Barnes.

For all the years he was in the band, Len spoke of a child that he rigorously denied to be his, saying that at the time of conception he wasn't the lone suitor. To avoid what he considered unfair maintenance for the child, he even had two possible fathers subpoenaed in court. He lost the case and dutifully, but reluctantly, supported his son until the lad became sixteen years of age. A short while after Len's death, John received a telephone call from a young man in Leicestershire, who believed the clarinettist had known his father, and asking for any information he might be able to pass on. With a degree of trepidation, John agreed to meet him, and on deciding a method of identification, arranged a rendezvous at St Pancras station. As John stood on the platform, a young Lennie Hastings walked towards him...

CHAPTER EIGHT

GENTLEMEN OF PLEASURE

The gale subsided, to be followed by a short period of calm before the next guest breezed into our lives in the shape of Earl Hines, the acknowledged 'Fatha' of the modern jazz piano.

Earl was accompanied by his wife and two young daughters, and he had taken a short lease on an apartment in Kensington, near the Albert Hall. I was anxious to meet him as he had long been a hero of mine, from his recordings with the Louis Armstrong All Stars.

Earl 'Fatha' Hines and a young clean-shaven guitarist

Like the others before him, his attire was immaculate, if perhaps a little dated in style. When he unbuttoned his black gabardine overcoat, he revealed a smart cherry-red polo-necked sweater and a pair of really high-draped trousers. His face beamed in a broad grin, showing well-cared-for teeth with an occasional glint of gold, clamping a well-smoked pipe that emitted the unmistakeable aroma of American tobacco. I think, but can't swear, that his face was lightly dusted with a subtle cosmetic and on his head he sported a well-groomed, but slightly obvious toupee. A little scar ran vertically across one of his eyes, which appeared to be slightly cloudier than the other. Having in later life had cataracts removed from both my eyes, I believe he may have been enduring the same misfortune. On reaching to shake his hand in introductory greeting, I saw on his right pinkie finger a beautiful diamond signet ring fashioned into the letters E H.

The Sports Guild for the occasion had hired a beautiful Steinway grand piano. As soon as he had played a few arpeggios, I thought to myself how much I was going to enjoy playing with him. Right from the first number, it became obvious that he had taken to Ron and Len. His broad grin in the bassist's direction proved that.

The structure of the sessions was obviously going to be different from that of the previous stars. It soon became obvious that, although he was a great band player and accompanist, his genius shone through in his solo masterpieces. The evening started as usual, with the band playing a few numbers (how Fred enjoyed that piano!) before welcoming Earl to the stand. After playing a song or two, usually his own compositions, such as Rosetta, Monday Date, or You Can Depend on Me, with the full ensemble, the maestro played a couple with the rhythm section before enthralling the spellbound audience with his solo magnificence. I remember his version of Duke Ellington's Sophisticated Lady bringing rapturous applause from the hushed room and tears to your author's eyes.

His final solo was St Louis Blues. After stating the melody of what I consider to be one of the best blues ever written, Earl gradually brought his improvisation to a rocking climax by holding an octave on his thumb and third finger of his right hand, while building a crescendo of open chords with his left. Suddenly a handkerchief appeared in his left hand and he began to mop his brow. All the time this right hand kept the incessant octaves driving on.

"Help! I need help! Ron Mathewson! Lennie Hastings! Jim Douglas! John Barnes! Roy Williams! Alex Welsh!" and one by one, we would re-take our place on the stand and join him in bringing the evening to an unforgettable close. Or not quite! Earl had the perfect encore with the song 'It's a Pity to Say Goodnight', sung in his own inimitable style. What an experience!

Night after night, town after town, audience after audience, the experience of playing with Earl rewrote my personal history book. From City Halls to the Mansion House of the Dublin Mayor, to Osterley Rugby Club, it was the same wonderful deal.

My personal memory is of euphoria, tinged with deep despair and warm friendship. The despair came in the middle of a tour, which required travelling from my family home near Edinburgh to Huddersfield Town Hall. On arrival, I was met by a policeman, who informed me of the sudden death of my brother, Dick, in a road accident in Milan. I of course missed some days of the tour by returning home.

My friendship with the Hines family was cemented by a mild flirtation with his nineteen-year-old daughter, who returned the affection with a little kiss and cuddle one night, when Ron Mathewson and I were baby-sitting her and her younger sister, to allow their parents an evening out.

The final euphoric experience came in the form of a recording session for Fontana, on which Len, Ron, John, Alex and I were featured with Earl. The album, although dubiously named 'Jazz Means Hines', is a very good representation of the great pianist's visits to our shores and I for one am very proud to have been part of them.

At the end of the tour, Earl took the band for a meal in a good restaurant in Manchester, along with Jack, Jenks and Betty, and John and Eunice Pye, from the Sports Guild. On our return to the office, we were met by Jenks's German Shepherd guard dog barking loudly.

"Don't worry," said Jenks, "he's just frightened."

"He's frightened? I'm so frightened, I almost turned white!" replied the shaken pianist.

Earl returned for another tour, this time when Ron Rae was with the band. If anything, the rhythm section was better, probably partly because we knew what to expect this time, and partly because we were getting a little more used to touring with such great idols of jazz. Don't get me wrong, please, I don't want to give the impression of familiarity breeding contempt, I am merely trying to convey a feeling of more security amongst the members of the band and a glorious feeling of anticipation of what lay before us.

What times! What memories!

Gentleman, Anglophile, Lawrence 'Bud' Freeman, one of the famous Austin High Gang, and member of the Chicagoans, was probably most revered for his work with his own band, Summa Cum Laude, and his wonderful compositions, such as 'The Eel', from that period. Looking for all the world like a stereotype city bank manager, Bud personified dapperness. From his shiny bald pate to his beautifully manicured fingers, he portrayed the English Gentleman like a picture from The Tatler magazine. To complete the illusion, he was dressed in a hand-made, button-down shirt, and military-style tie, razor-sharp creased beige gabardine trousers, shining tan brogues, and an expensive pure wool Harris Tweed sports jacket, with the mandatory silk handkerchief in the breast pocket. Above his top lip, which was spread wide to reveal gleaming teeth with a sensuous gap between the front upper incisors, nestled a short, thin, beautifully clipped moustache of the sort favoured by famous film stars of the thirties and forties, such as Clark Gable, Roland Gilbert, etc. He greeted us with a slight chuckle in his voice with the words, "I've heard so much about you guys, it's so nice to be home."

Looking back, I think Bud tried so hard to cultivate his Anglophile image, that at some stage he really did begin to believe he was a native of these islands. There was nothing English about his playing, however. Here was one of the innovators of the tenor saxophone in jazz music; a man who had inspired generations of musicians throughout the world. Three great players in their own right with whom I had the pleasure of playing, Eddie Miller, Zoot Sims, and our own Danny Moss, all owed some of their style to him. I believe 'Prez', himself, the superb Lester Young, was influenced by Bud in his formative years and didn't mind admitting so!

Bud and the band in the studios

It was obvious from the start that this was going to be musically different because Bud had a set programme he used on his world tours, and intended using it with us. While jamming with the whole ensemble, he improvised freely but, for his features, he used the same numbers in the same order, even playing the same solos, at every concert. To an audience who would hear his performance once, or at most, a couple of times, this didn't matter too much but, to me, the repetition began to get a little wearing, especially after three or four tours. One of the tunes he liked to play was, 'Exactly Like You', in which he quoted from another great standard, "Early Autumn'.

Before continuing with this anecdote, it would be appropriate to tell you a little more about the character of the man. Bud loved the Sport of Kings or, rather, liked to have a little daily flutter on the nags. However I must reveal that, like most gamblers I've met, with the exception of poor old Lennie, he was less than honest about his success as a punter – he never seemed to lose! Then we discovered his secret method: before leaving for a gig, Bud would purchase the late afternoon edition of the London Evening Standard, which published the results of the early race meetings. Thus, furnished with the relevant information, he would relay his list of winners to the amazed band chaps, hot from the press and straight from the horses' mouths, so to speak. One of his genuine successes was a horse named Larkhill, which returned odds of four-to-one. As it happened, we were due to make a recording the next morning for Fontana, as the next in the series. At one stage, Bud informed the engineer that we were to record a number co-composed by Fred and himself. When asked the title, Bud shamelessly replied that it was called 'Larkhill 4-to-1'. He then launched into his quote from 'Early Autumn' to the chord sequence of 'Exactly Like You'.

Although I believe Bud genuinely respected and enjoyed our company, both musically and personally, he never appeared happier than when in a large company of admirers, especially when there were plenty of critics and VIPs among them. As he talked and answered questions about himself and famous people he knew, his eyes darted about looking for someone in the latter category. For example, when we stayed in a hotel in the Mount Pleasant area of Liverpool, the band call had been set for six o'clock. I happened to leave my room at the same time as the tenor star and immediately struck up a conversation. On entering the crowded Lounge Bar (which boasted, amongst others, members of the great Merseysippi Band), he immediately changed the subject, and in a voice some decibels higher, announced, "and so he said, BUD FREEMAN, you'll..." or something to that effect, as if anyone in the bar could have failed to recognise him, or spot the saxophone he was carrying.

Another occasion saw us as part of a presentation at London's Royal Festival Hall, this time as a band in our own right. I remember Errol Garner being on the bill, and Bud was with a trio. Milling about in the Artists' Bar, we were spotted by the maestro. Flinging his arms around Fred (but still looking over his shoulder), he said, "Freddie, you were wonderful!"

Before Fred could quite utter that we hadn't played yet, he cut across, "You'll be wonderful!"

What a man. Unflappable!

But, in the end you had to forgive him his little eccentricities, even cheating at golf, which he did by concealing a similarly marked ball to the one he was playing in his trouser waistband, to be dropped down the inside of his trouser leg if the original ball appeared to be lost. I can picture him on the stand now, gently rocking to and fro in time to the music, his foot gently tapping in sympathetic accompaniment.

He accepted our menial transport, even though the glove compartment door rapped his knee every time Fred hit a bump! He even travelled back to London in the Lenvan, piloted by an inebriated drummer, and reminded where he was by the bass nudging the back of his head from time to time. No wonder he incessantly asked, "Do we fly to Morden or wherever?" in the American way. I never saw him less than immaculately attired in his Harris tweed jacket, cavalry twill trousers, Simpson of Piccadilly shirts, and highly polished brogues. He rarely perspired, as if the process had been banned from his utopian existence.

Nevertheless, I can't help feeling that Anglophile, would-be Thespian, great saxophonist, Lawrence 'Bud' Freeman was a bit of a little-boy-lost, somewhat of a loner and, perhaps, a slight misfit in the brash world of the professional jazz musician.

I grew to like him very much. He taught me a lot about musical scales, especially the use of the whole tone in jazz, and although I found his solos repetitive, I gained great satisfaction from playing with him.

Not to be outdone by Wild Bill, I became his Scottish nephew (notice the obvious generation gap). At least once a night he would say to me, "Jum Dooglas, ye'll mak a mullion poonds!" in a terrible Scottish accent. He was wrong there though: I never have, and probably never will!

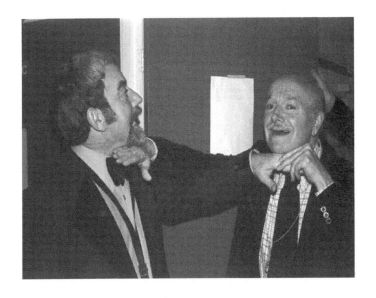

John Barnes hitting it off with Bud Freeman

CHAPTER NINE

TRANSPORTS OF DELIGHT

The biggest problem facing any band leader in Alex's day, was finding an economical method of transporting his musicians and their instruments to and from engagements.

Nowadays most of them ask their men to split up into as few personal cars as possible, share the expenses, and make their own way to the gig. The leader usually tries to find a little extra money to help, by adding a small expenses fee to the contract. This is fine, if the performers constitute a big enough attraction to enable the promoter to charge a little more at the door. The obvious drawbacks to this method of travelling are the possibilities of the musicians, through breakdowns or geographical misinformation, arriving at best, late or, at worst, failing to arrive at all, although the modern use of mobile phones and 'satnavs' has largely negated this worry.

When I joined the band, roads were of the single carriageway type and vehicles, as a result, moved much more slowly. It was considered advisable to travel together in some sort of van, bus, or wagon. You bought or hired some sort of windowless delivery truck, non-insulated against condensation, and governed by a forty miles per hour speed limit, to which you did your best to fit windows, aircraft seats etc. Or, you rented a commercial Dormobile (in the days before the Transit), into which you squeezed as many men and instruments as possible, leaving the larger equipment to survive the elements, strapped to a roof rack.

Alex had plumped for the former in the shape of a former Post Office parcel delivery van. Looking back, it must have been reasonably luxurious for the time, with its aircraft seats (complete with safety straps), and luggage space at the rear.

I had actually travelled in this vehicle prior to my joining the band when guitarist, Tony Pitt, had offered to put me up at his flat after a party. It was nearly my last trip in any van. On the way home, just at Ealing Common, Tony fell asleep. Seeing a lamppost approaching me at an all too uncomfortable speed, I yelled out. Tony yanked the steering wheel to the right, narrowly avoiding a head-on collision, and thus perhaps saving our lives. The van suffered extensive damage and, although repaired, was never quite the same again. Slowly it became more and more of a liability. The passenger door, economically repaired, leaked in an unbearable draught, and the heater had long since stopped functioning at its true capacity and rattled noisily. To counteract the cold, the musicians had bought sleeping bags, into which, larva-like, they snuggled, fastened to the chin, while the driver strapped them into their seats. Warm to a degree at last, you would be just about to drop off to sleep when, *splosh*, a freezing cold drop of condensation from the unlined roof would land right in your eye.

Thankfully that particular van's days were numbered. The final straw that broke the legendary camel's back was two incidents of brake failure, one on the A12 where we went straight over a roundabout, and the second when we failed to stop, approaching a red light at a crossroads in Sale, near Manchester. It had to go after that. But what could we find to replace it? Money was tight and vehicles of the size and comfort required were expensive. Fred came up with a short-term solution. He knew a friend of a friend who owned a similar sized vehicle that he hired out with himself as driver. Enter Mr Feet!

I suppose it was his height and lankiness that made Victor's head, hands, and feet look out of proportion with the rest of his frame but, in truth, they were unusually large. I don't have particularly small hands, but I remember how his engulfed mine when, on introduction, we shook each other's. There was an indefinable angularity about his entire bearing. His head, crowned with dark, wavy, Brylcreemed hair, stuck out of his collar at the end of a long thin neck. His large ears were of the variety favoured by Toby-jugs, while his long thin nose with its flared nostrils cut the air, reminiscent of a cow-catcher on an American locomotive. His fleshy mouth opened frequently to emit a high-pitched chortle, which completely belied his stature. But it was his digital and pedal extremities that struck you the most. The hands, which I have already partly described, were joined to long thin arms by bony wrists, which protruded from a much-too-short-sleeved corduroy jacket. His fingers, also long and bony with large knuckles, fan-like, completely covered the steering wheel they manipulated. He favoured beige cavalry twill trousers to encase his long thin legs, which were bisected by obviously knobbly knees, sticking out, as did his elbows, at an angle of forty-five degrees. Holding all this up were platforms one and two of Paddington Station. Encased in two, tan-coloured leather suitcases were a pair of the biggest plates of meat I've ever seen! As he walked, they scythed the air, destroying everything that got in their way. Ants and beetles for miles around packed their bags and fled when they heard he was in their vicinity!

Imagine then, if you will, this apparition performing a tango. He did. With Brenda Hunt. I saw them. At the Zetland Hotel, in Redcar. I have hardly seen anything funnier! As they danced, his head jerked up and down and from side to side, and his elbows became lethal weapons, threatening immediate destruction to any object or person careless enough to get in their way. One huge hand covered his partner's entire back, while the other swallowed her complete right hand and forearm. All the time, his size-twenties were eating up acres of dance floor; pendulum-like, they swung to and fro like a pair of out-of-control fairground swing boats. Oblivious to it all, Brenda smiled benignly while the band collapsed in tears of laughter.

Occasionally, his un-age-able mother, and their German shepherd dog, accompanied Victor. His mother's appearance was the antithesis of his own, hers short and dumpy, to his long and thin. Swathed from head to foot in a luxurious fur coat and matching hat, regardless of season or weather, she spoke with a cracking, cackling, Cockney accent. With the dog beside her, she perched on the front seat of the van; from a distance it was nigh impossible to tell them apart. In my imagination, I can picture the two of them, mother and dog, Aleutian-like, by a fishing hole cut in a frozen Alaska lake, while Victor performs a frantic 'buck and wing' in an effort to keep warm.

Vic's van, as I have already intimated, was another converted delivery truck. There was an extra side door, though, as well as the normal rear and passenger doors and Vic had built a partition towards the rear, creating a luggage compartment. This is where we stored the larger, bulkier instruments. The side door afforded entry into the sitting room, for that's what it was! On the far right, up against the partition, stood a wardrobe, in which we hung the band suits. In the middle of the floor, surrounded by a small, three-piece-suite and various scatter cushions, was a coffee table, garnished with ashtrays, magazines and a deck of playing cards. A couple of occasional chairs had somehow also been squeezed in to accommodate the numbers. Victor had thought of everything, except one, that is – he hadn't anchored the furniture to the floor. Off we went, out of the mews, slowly into the Cromwell Road, gently through the traffic lights and over Hammersmith flyover to Chiswick roundabout. Then, disaster struck! We had just settled down to a nice game of cards, when the furniture started to waltz around the floor on its castors. By the time we straightened out on the M4 motorway, we all had different hands of cards! Travel sick and bruised, we alighted a few hours later in Bristol. There just had to be a better way than this...

Lennie Hastings offered one solution. Fed up with travelling home every evening in all weathers on a moped, he had long considered getting himself a little van. Two things stood in his way: firstly, he never had any money and, secondly, he didn't hold a full driving licence. His suggestion was that, if the band paid for driving lessons, he would find enough money to buy a second-hand vehicle. A little reluctantly, Alex agreed.

Fred's wife, Brenda (she of the tango), had been married before to a second-hand car dealer from Palmers Green. Douglas Gower and his second wife, June, had remained close friends with Fred and Brenda, and were regular visitors to the

Fishmongers' Arms on a Sunday night. Doug just happened to have a nice little runner, a 5cwt Ford Thames van, on his lot that Len could have for fifty quid. Len borrowed the money and took delivery.

As it happened, I was also receiving driving instruction at that time, so it was decided that one of us should apply for an early test in order that he could legally supervise the other. In the meantime, we would take a chance and travel together with the heavy equipment in the 'Len-van', as it soon became known. Fred, in the interim, acquired a reasonable Zephyr Zodiac from the same source. This would transport the rest of the chaps.

Almost from the word go, it appeared that the Len-van was a bit of a pig in a poke. There was difficulty in starting the engine, and when we did get it running, an ominous 'knocking' emanated from somewhere below. It also seemed to need a lot of oil. Its first test was just around the corner, on the approaching Saturday, in fact: a trip to The Digbeth Civic Centre in Birmingham. After filling the tank with petrol and checking the oil level, Len and I set off. Everything seemed fine as we drove northward through London and out on to the M1. There was the usual rattling and knocking, of course, but nothing out of the ordinary. Len drove, while I supervised. Just south of what is now Junction 13 on the M1, the inevitable happened. The engine gave a loud bang, followed by clouds of smoke and steam from under the bonnet. We rolled to a stop on the hard shoulder.

The Len-van

"Just needs a bit more oil," said Herr Len. "Lift the bonnet and let's have a gander."

Checking the mark on the dipstick, he reached for the oil can.

"I wouldn't bother doing that," I exclaimed from the prone position I had adopted by the nearside front wheel. A pool of oil was rapidly forming on the ground, as it poured from a hole in the engine. A piston big-end had gone. Fortunately, we were within walking distance of a garage, the proprietor of which towed us in. After assessing the repair and agreeing to complete it by the next evening, Mr Charlesworth (for that was his name,

I recall), offered to drive us and the equipment to the gig, and thus save the day. The repair and hire, of course, took care of the engagement fee, but at least we made it on time.

Next door to the garage, there was a used-car parts depot, where wrecks from the motorway were stacked high, and I wouldn't mind betting that's where the crankshaft and pistons that went into the Len-van's engine came from. Nevertheless, the next day we were mobile again, but that wasn't the end of it. When the engine had lost its oil it had overheated, and in the process warped the cylinder head. Within days, the hot water circulating around the engine blew the head gasket, necessitating a replacement. This occurred several times before we were able to eventually have the head skimmed.

It wasn't long before we both passed our driving tests, but not before another remarkable event worth recalling took place, this time on the way to Newark in Nottinghamshire.

Just north of Norman Cross on the A1, in what was and now is once more, Rutland, cruising at a steady sixty miles per hour with Lennie at the wheel, the Len-van was overtaken by a leather-clad Police Officer on a motorbike. Waving us into an adjacent lay-by, he dismounted and strolled towards us.

"Are you the owner of this vehicle and do you have your driving licence?" he enquired of our ashen-faced Fuehrer. Len produced his provisional document. Entering its details in his notebook, the copper said, "This van should travel at no more than forty miles per hour, and I recorded you as doing in excess of sixty. You will be hearing from us."

Without further ado, he remounted his bike and rode off. He never once asked for proof of my authority as co-driver. Inevitably, sometime later, Lennie received the anticipated summons and notification of a fine, which required him to submit his driving licence for endorsement. Together with his guilty plea, and a cheque to cover the fine, he forwarded his moped licence. It was duly endorsed and returned!

To be truthful, both the Len-van and the Fred-mobile had long since seen better days. They were forever breaking down or failing to start. It became commonplace to pass one or the other in a lay-by, its bonnet raised and its driver hunched over the engine.

The weekend we appeared at the Chateau Impney, the wonderful folly in Staffordshire, was no exception. Billed as a jazz weekend, the occasion was well attended and the hotel manager and staff, as a mark of appreciation, treated the band as VIPs, wining and dining us very well. When it came time for us to leave on the Sunday afternoon, the entire staff came to wave us off. With the instruments and personal luggage packed into the vehicles and the chaps installed in their seats, the two drivers prepared to start the engines. Firstly, it was the turn of the Zodiac. Nothing! All hands to the pumps, as we pushed to jump-start it. Success! Then came the turn of the Len-van to be given the same, fortunately successful, treatment. Slightly embarrassed, but accustomed to the situation, the band finally departed. With the hotel staff waving their farewells, the two wrecks left the car park, the exhaust pipe of the Len-van replying in a similar fashion.

On another occasion, while en-route to Norwich one rainy Friday, in the middle of the rush-hour, stuck in a two-mile tailback, someone ran into the back of us. The double bass (which travelled on its side taking up the entire length of the van with its neck dividing driver and passenger, partially depriving one's sight of the other), shot forward, hitting me on the back of the head, and, in the process, ripping the passenger seat from its moorings on the floor. From that moment on, if you placed your head between your knees, you could see the road rushing underneath the vehicle through the hole in the floor.

But it wasn't only Len and I who suffered at the hands of the Len-van. To enable him to get home to Luton, Roy sometimes borrowed it. As he set off northwards one evening after a gig, everything seemed fine. Following at some distance on the same route, John suddenly came across Roy standing by the van, scratching his head and staring at a flat tyre. Stopping to offer assistance, John walked over to the vehicle to find out what was wrong.

Roy pointed to the jack. "It doesn't seem to be working," he said. Kneeling down, John started to wind the handle, but the wheels remained on the ground. Then they noticed the body of the van; it had gone up with the jack, leaving the wheels behind!

At this point, it may be advisable to describe the Len-van in all its glory. It was a small, blue Ford Thames delivery van with a 100E side-valve engine, two side and double rear doors, and the bonnet and wings from the 'Popular' range. Two side windows in the doors afforded a limited view to the driver, as did two small rear ones. It had wing mirrors – a godsend when the interior was full. Unfortunately, time had made its mark. The once gleaming paintwork had turned a grimy matt, one of the rear windows had lost its glass (thanks to the bass spike), and the rear door handle had long since ceased to lock, and indeed had developed a habit of opening itself. To make amends, a square of cardboard had been fitted in the rear window frame and a wire coat hanger twisted around the handle and secured to the upper left side hinge, preventing it from opening. Because of its air of battle fatigue and its eye-patch window, it was known for a while as Moshe Dayan, in all deference to the great Israeli General. Having described the villain of the piece, it would now seem appropriate to set the scene of the next act in our 'Travels with a Len-van'.

Luton is geographically placed at the junction of two Roman roads: Watling Street and Icknield Way, on the edge of the Chiltern Hills. Roads to and from town are of a hilly nature and the streets in the centre are similar. One either drives up or down to Luton, depending on one's approach. Wellington Street, the scene of our next escapade, is no exception. Nowadays of course, as the modern trait dictates, it has become a non-parking, one-way thoroughfare, but in the sixties it was a two-way, narrow street with parking allowed on both its sides, making driving a lottery at the best of times, and a nightmare on a busy Saturday morning.

The unfortunate hero was Roy, who, using the borrowed van to his advantage and taking the chance to do some shopping, was looking for somewhere to park. Feeding into the main thoroughfare, George Street, are several streets all running parallel with each other: Castle Street, George Street West, King Street, and Wellington Street. In an attempt to park, Roy was threading his way up and down the streets in turn and had just turned to ascend the latter. With a string of cars behind him and others facing him waiting to descend, the worst happened! Without warning, the coat hanger wire securing the rear doors snapped. The doors flew open and Len's drums rolled down the hill, chased by a red-faced Royston.

I could go on and on. The tales of the Len-van are endless. When a policeman in Huddersfield informed the drummer that he had bought a stolen vehicle, for example, or the time he was prosecuted for 'driving with dangerous parts', etc. How many would you like?

To bring down the curtain on the Len-van, I will recount one last tale - probably the best.

The Government's introduction of the 'breathalyser' brought another set of problems for the travelling musician. Virtually unable to perform without a stiff drink or two and, because of his residential isolation from the rest of the band, Len had to, at some point of the evening, possibly face being pulled up and tested. Although, by this time the Len-van was no longer used to transport the drums, he had to drive to and from his home in Twickenham to the pick-up point, usually at Pennant Mews in Earls' Court where both Alex and Fred rented flats. Harvey Weston had joined the band by this time and had negotiated the contract hire of a brand new Ford Transit minibus, in which the entire band and their instruments could travel together.

On the night of our tale, the band was playing at 'The Fish'. To minimise the breathalyser risk, Lennie had arranged to journey from the Mews to and from the gig in Fred's car, leaving only the relatively short distance to drive home. Here is the story, as recounted by Fred:

"We arrived back at The Mews pretty late, having had a few after the performance. As we were pretty tired, Brenda and I went straight upstairs and were undressing for bed, when we heard Len get into the van and turn the ignition key. Whirr, whirr, whirr went the starter motor – no joy – nothing. Whirr, whirr, whirr; it was as dead as a dodo. Next we heard the sound of the bonnet being raised and the tinkering and fiddling with wires, etc, before it was slammed back down. Whirr, whirr,

whirr, wheeeeeeerrrrr; the battery had started to fade. Just then a window opened and a head poked out.

"Do you mind, we are trying to get some sleep?" an angry voice cried.

"I'm f***ing trying to get f***ing home!" replied Herr Splutz. "F*** off!"

The silence was followed by the sound of straining, grunting, and groaning, as the lifeless vehicle was pushed to the far end of The Mews.

Whirr, whirr, wheeerrrr, whebang! Splutter, splutter! Brrroom, brrroom!

The engine exploded into life and our hero was mobile and roared off along the Cromwell Road.

The phone rang.

"What the bloody hell was all that about?" asked Alex.

Laughing fit to burst, I tried to explain."

Eventually, of course, the Len-van died. It was replaced by a saloon version of the same model and manufacture, which, I seem to recall, presented Len with an identical set of problems. However, etched forever in my memory is the picture of an immaculate Herr Hastings, standing proudly at the door of a gleaming Len-van (no doubt washed, cleaned and polished by his lovely, long-suffering wife, Janet), prior to our driving to Southampton docks where we were due to embark on a

Mediterranean cruise. Indeed, I have a photograph I took on the occasion. See for yourself.

But things were to improve with the eventual contract hire of a brand new vehicle and even a driver, as I will describe in a later chapter.

Brian Lemon and me boarding the bus

CHAPTER TEN

FORBIDDEN FRUIT

When we learned that our next tour was to be with Count Basie sideman and trombonist, Dickie Wells, and the first part of it in Switzerland, we were filled with a mixture of excitement and cautious curiosity. In the first place, a rumour had reached us that the great trombone player hardly ever played because of his being a recovering alcoholic. We were reassured that he was practising regularly in anticipation of the trip, and that we need have no worries about his drinking, as he hadn't touched a drop for months or even years.

On our introduction at London's famous Marquee Club, I was immediately struck by his quiet charm and slightly wearied good looks. He was tall and slim with spaniel-like brown eyes, and sported a pencil moustache above his mouthpiece-bruised top lip. A Burberry-style raincoat was open to reveal a navy blazer and grey slacks. On his close-cropped curly hair perched a pork pie hat. I was reminded of tales I'd heard of him, and trumpeter Buck Clayton (in Billie Holliday's words, the handsomest man she'd ever seen), when they shared the stand with the Count. In one hand he held a sheaf of musical arrangements, and in the other a leather wallet containing his horn.

He was sober!

The music we rehearsed that day became features of the band's repertoire in the following years. Dickie's great version of 'Between the Devil and the Deep Blue Sea', which had highlighted the wonderful Django Reinhardt, Duke Ellington's 'It Don't Mean a Thing', and his own tribute to his personal inspiration, Tommy Dorsey, 'Bones for the King', were all incorporated into the band's library. As a solo number, he chose 'Somewhere Over the Rainbow', on which he favoured his famous pepper-pot mute, which at one stage he gave to Roy Williams and which eventually ended up, I believe, in the possession of the late, lamented Campbell Burnap.

So off we went to Switzerland. Night after night, concert after concert, the performances improved as we became more familiar with the arrangements. But, it was a short-lived fool's paradise. A rather attractive hotel receptionist, obviously taken in by Dickie's persuasive charm, had accepted his invitation to lunch with him. Completely unaware of his problem, and, while ordering lunch in a language unfamiliar to him, the lady had included a bottle of wine. The temptation was too great and Dickie accepted a glass or two with inevitable, disastrous, consequences.

The first signs of an impending catastrophe manifested themselves that same evening at about six o'clock, when we were enjoying an early meal before leaving for the concert. I was quietly enjoying a good steak when our hero appeared, none too steady, at the bottom of the staircase that led up to the rooms. Staggering towards my table, he stopped and, without a murmur, reached down to my plate. Sliding his right hand under my steak, while at the same time picking up a grilled tomato, he directed my meal to his open mouth. Unfortunately, his hand-to-mouth co-ordination had gone for a Burton, and he ended up, much to my bewildered amazement and amusement, planting the soft fruit clown-like on his nose, while all the time, beef juices ran down his chin on to his clothes. He was plastered!

Searching both himself and his room, we found a bottle of brandy. After several cups of strong, black coffee he was just about able to make the concert, but it was the beginning of the end. The cunning of the alcoholic manifested itself in his secreting bottles in unlikely places. We even removed a bottle of Cognac from a bag of fruit. For the rest of the tour, fruit was forbidden.

By the time we left Switzerland, Dickie had become an embarrassment to us all, so it was with great relief that we watched him escorted back to his hotel by an agency representative when we arrived home at Heathrow Airport. Dickie had the last word, or rather action, though, after managing to get himself locked into a lavatory and having to be rescued by one of the band.

But what about the British part of the tour that he had been contracted to undertake? Alex put his foot down, insisting that he must be dried out and chaperoned by the agency at all times. Indeed this was the case and the *status quo* returned. Until we went to Hastings, that is: the historic town was about to host another battle.

On the day in question, no one at the office was available to ferry Dickie to the gig and, to be truthful, as he had been behaving impeccably once more, John Barnes offered to pick up the trombonist from his hotel and bring him to Hastings. When they arrived slightly late, John's first words were, "He's drunk."

A nightmare scenario then unfolded. After a couple of numbers from the band, jazz and blues critic and writer, the late Derek Stewart Baxter, mounted the stand to introduce Dickie. Alex counted us into 'Devil', and after an interesting intro from the trombonist, we finished the great arrangement to polite applause. After a couple of equally disastrous offerings, Alex decided it was time for Dickie's feature, 'Over the Rainbow'. Following an eight-bar intro from Fred, we were off, or rather, the trombone slide was. It was plain to everyone that the unfortunate fellow was having difficulty re-uniting the two parts of the instrument, and seeing his plight, Roy jumped on to the stage to be of assistance.

"Outta mah way, boy!" yelled Dickie, wildly swinging his arms and fists at his would-be benefactor. The music came to a full stop and the curtains closed. Derek went to the front of the stage to apologise, uttering the sad and, in my opinion, slightly cruel words, "How disappointing it is to find one's idol has feet of clay!"

We finished what remained of the concert without him, and different guests replaced him for the rest of the scheduled tour. Dickie returned to the States and to his job as a messenger for one of the large department stores.

On the positive side, a session at the Dancing Slipper Club in Nottingham was recorded by Alan Gilmour, or 'Marconi' as we called him, and has been issued on Jazzology. It's very listenable and an example of his playing at its best.

There is a footnote, however, in its own way interesting, if not a little touching. For years afterwards, indeed until death with its finality intervened, Alex and Dickie corresponded by letter, exchanging Christmas cards, and used visiting musicians to carry verbal messages to one another. Alex, of course, was also alcoholic, but was never affected by his problem in the way Dickie had been, and maintained his dignity in the public eye right to the end. Although he never said a word about it, he

must at times have felt, *there but for the Grace of God, go I.*
Maybe it does take one to know one, as the saying goes.

Life is strange.

But the guests kept coming and tours became longer.

Former Ellington sideman, chain smoker, author, and
trumpet player, Rex Stewart, arrived with his daughter and
another dinky pork pie hat, but without his chops. By this time,
exciting as it was, I could detect a little ennui running through
the band. Not travel fatigue, but a suggestion that it would be
nice to just get a few gigs without guests, with all due respect to
the legends. After all, we had not long formed before all this
started, of course, and had ideas and plans of our own.

Rex, as I say, hadn't played a lot in the period before he
joined us, and apart from his great singing, relied on the band to
carry him until such time as he got his lip in. On the plus side,
he was a very well-read conversationalist and brought with him
some great memories of his time with the great big bands. So
the tour continued without, in my opinion, ever reaching the
dizzy heights of the earlier ones, except for two notable
occasions.

The first was in the form of a concert organised by the late
Jack Higgins, to take place in the American Embassy Building in
Grosvenor Square, London. Without any planning or
rehearsing Rex decided to present the audience with a 'History
of Jazz', opening with yours truly playing a solo version of
Swanee River on the banjo. Fine, you might think, but not for

me! For a start, I was nervous of being on the stage alone, and secondly not convinced that I was adept enough as a solo banjoist to do justice to even such a simple song. Arthur Bell and John Barleycorn came to my rescue. With both in attendance, my effort and, indeed, the whole concert, were successful and the format worked well.

So well, in fact, that Rex decided to incorporate parts of it in our shows, especially his 'Shouting the Blues'. We were booked to appear on ITV's, 'A Whole Lot Going On', introduced by Cathy McGowan and Barry Fantoni, and featuring Georgie Fame and Eric Burden of the Animals R&B group. During the rehearsals, Eric, backed by Georgie, started to sing a bluesy number. Without warning Rex suddenly jumped up, and walking into the middle of the studio, began to shout the blues in the style of the early pioneers of the idiom. Finishing with a "That's the Blues!" he re-joined us on our set.

Eddie Miller had long been admired by Alex for his fine work with the great Bob Crosby's 'Bobcats', and probably more so for his great tenor saxophone playing with Matty Mattlock in the film, 'Pete Kelly's Blues'. Bringing him over for a tour was perhaps a little more risky than normal, because of his being less well-known to the fringe fans. We need not have worried, of course. His playing suited the band to a T, and the audiences, getting used to the high standards of performances, took to him well. Although he relegated the wonderful Al Gay to the clarinettist's chair, the band played as a great unit. Eddie's ballads in particular were very poignant and moving, especially, I remember, "Body and Soul', 'Sophisticated Lady', and my favourite, 'Little Girl Blue' of which a version was recorded by 'Fontana' records and on which I had the honour to accompany him and share the solo.

I liked to listen to his stories of his early experiences before and after his wonderful career in Hollywood as a session musician. He liked nothing better than to relax with a small Scottish libation in the hotel after the concert and reminisce, sometimes with a slight degree of elaboration, but nonetheless enthralling.

Years after Alex was gone, I was pursuing a mixed career of playing and cooking when I was invited to appear as a replacement for the indisposed guitar legend, Nappy Lamare, at a concert by the famous 'South Rampart Street Paraders', in a Hastings Jazz Festival. I proudly took the stand with Yank Lawson, Abe Most, Eddie Miller, Bob Havens, Lou Stein, Bob Haggart, and Nick Fatool. What an experience! Unfortunately that was the last time I saw or played with Eddie. I later heard he had succumbed to Alzheimer's disease and passed away quietly.

It was a pleasure to know you, Eddie.

Having missed ever meeting Satchmo, and disappointed that one of his all-stars, Jack Teagarden, was too ill to tour, it had been wonderful to play with another in the form of Earl Hines. It was exciting to be informed that a third was to be our next guest. Michael 'Peanuts' Hucko was, of course, musically familiar to me in many ways: his wartime appearances with Glenn Miller, the wonderful Town Hall Concert, and his great recordings with Eddie Condon. Once again the tour was a success, musically and financially.

We found Peanuts charming and musically everything we had expected him to be. If there was one chink in his armour, only experienced in my role as the Black Knight, it was, like Bud, his reluctance to vary from his well-rehearsed programme, even refusing requests for favourites from the audience. Like Red and Ruby, he liked guitar and so featured me often. A recording on Lake Records, from a transcript of a session in Nottingham, proves this to a degree. I think it is one of the best representations of these great times we have. Alex and Maggie became great friends with Peanuts and his lovely wife, Louise. When Alex died, Maggie received a heartwarming letter from them, which she cherishes.

Since those days, I have played several times with Peanuts, both home and abroad and, although perhaps a little weary of the repetitive repertoire, I enjoyed myself immensely. He, too, is now gone, of course. There must be some great sessions up there!

Before I am accused of turning this chapter into a name dropping exercise, I will brag about just a few more of the guests we had the pleasure of accompanying on single concerts and recordings: Ben Webster, Albert Nicholas, Matty Mattlock,

Bill Coleman, Pee Wee Erwin, Johnnie Mince, Willie 'The Lion' Smith, Sammy Price, Vic Dickenson, Yank Lawson, Wingy Manone, Clark Terry, Stephane Grappelli; if I have missed any, may they forgive me.

It's not a name-dropping exercise - just the thrill of being fortunate enough to have been in the right band at the right time and the joy of playing with my heroes.

Jim, Roy, Alex, Roger, John, Pete and Brian

Jim, Roy Fred, John, Roger, Alex, Phil Finch (roady), and Pete in foreground

Jim and Brian

Alex and Maggie arriving in Jersey

Jim, Roy, and Al

John and Roger

Jim and Alex

Dick Cary and Roy

Roy and Spike Milligan

John and Spike

Alex and Spike

Roy with Spike 'Stand-in'

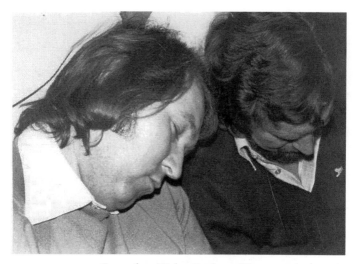

Somnulent Mickey Cooke and Jim

Roger and Jim

Barney Bates

Pete and Jim

Thirsty Work!

Roger, Brian, and The Invisible Man

Everyone's a Drummer

Alex and Jeff Garrard

Jack Peacock, 'Pop' Robson, Jim and Jeff

Where did you get that hat?

Jack, John, Roy and Pat Barnes

...and so to bed...

CHAPTER ELEVEN

BULL FIDDLE AND THE IVORY TICKLER

When Ronnie Rae decided his future was back in Scotland, Alex was faced with a dilemma, which, for a short time, grew horns. It wasn't a shortage of good bass players that was the problem but, rather, finding one mentally strong enough and with enough volume to withstand the incessant metronomic pounding of Len's bass drum pedal. All of them fine players in their own right, Tony Baylis (who came with us to Newport), Gerry Higgins (on the Wild Bill album), Dave Holland (who made a career with Miles Davis) and two Brian Joneses, all came and went.

The answer came with a former colleague of the drummer, in the form of Harvey Weston, a technically gifted player who *owned an amplifier.* An affable, trendy young man, married with two young boys, Harvey proved himself for the next few years to be the ideal man for the job. He readily fitted into the band's set up, even helping to calm the troubled waters between the leader and the 'Fuhrer' which had at times almost reached boiling point.

Harvey, always a follower of fashion, is a deep thinker, who betrays his innermost anxieties with a cheery countenance and a never-say-die outlook on life. A moderate drinker by nature, often leaving it entirely alone, he sometimes let his thinning hair down to become the life and soul of the party. Although artistic by nature, Harvey is also extremely practical, ensuring he always has both feet on the ground when it comes to common sense and responsibility. Even when times were hard, his home and family were a credit to him, and he somehow managed to find a little extra cash to indulge his hobby: motorcars.

I don't think he could believe his eyes when he discovered our *modus operandi* of transport: the old Ford Zodiac and the Len-van. His own car was a Volkswagen Beetle, in near immaculate condition, and tuned to perfection. Harvey is, as I have mentioned, very clever with his hands, whether it be drawing, working on car engines, or repairing musical instruments, which is nowadays responsible for a reasonable slice of his income.

At first he travelled with Lennie to be with his instruments but, sooner or later, I seem to recall, he was making his own way to gigs. But even Harvey, with all his knowledge, couldn't help on one occasion.

We had spent most of a Saturday and half of the Sunday in Stafford with a great friend of the band and his wife, Brian and Brenda Casson, and their large family. Brian is a jazz lover and trombonist, who, at that time, worked as a salesman for Besson Instruments. He had negotiated contracts to supply instruments for Alex and both Roys, as a form of advertising. On a regular basis, whenever we were in the vicinity, we would cram into his none-too-large house to save a hotel bill. We would, of course, stay up until the early hours, drinking and listening to records. It was on the aforementioned Sunday afternoon, in the early months of the year, when everything was wet from a recent thaw, that our tale takes place.

We'd had a couple of pints at the local pub, enjoyed lunch with the family, and were about to set off on our journey to the next engagement. Taking our seats in the vehicles, parked on the road by the house, we said our farewells. Lennie's van started straight away, but the Zodiac, although its battery was well charged, didn't give even a cough. Under the bonnet goes Harvey! Twenty minutes... half an hour... nothing!

"We had better send for the RAC," said Fred.

We all piled back into Brian's house to await the rescue service. After a short time a mechanical representative arrived and checked over the engine, still without success. By this time, Harvey was edging closer and closer to him, eventually ending up under the bonnet with the mechanic. Straightening up and stepping back, the befuddled engineer suddenly exploded: "Who's fixing this thing, you or me?" he enquired.

On another occasion, we broke down just outside Liverpool. After a heavy session at the Press Club, we had finally set off home at about five o'clock in the morning. Suddenly the engine died and Harvey said, "I think the accelerator return spring has broken at the carburettor."

This meant very little to most of us, and nothing at all to those who had already passed out. Under the bonnet went Harvey. About five minutes later the engine restarted and we were off home. I asked Harvey later where he had managed to find a spring at that time of the night.

"I just looked around the gutter and found a used condom. I used the ring like an elastic band and it worked fine. Don't ask me how it got there, but beggars can't be choosers."

Genius!

Harvey's bass playing was equal to his engineering. He uses a slightly different technique, involving a five-stringed instrument with a high C. This enables him to play chords, which he uses to great effect in his solos. Also, with the help of his small amplifier, he could be heard above Lennie's four-in-the-bar bass drum beat, which had, on occasion, driven both Ronnies crazy. Harvey can be heard to great effect on the Dresden recording, 'Alex Welsh in Concert', which many consider is our best album, notably his solo on, 'I Want a Little Girl'.

Alex put Harvey in charge of transport and it wasn't long before he came up trumps. As so often happened, one of the cars developed a problem just before a tour. Harvey knew of a van rental place in Wembley, and negotiated a deal on a long-term basis at a reasonable cost. This involved the use of one of the company's fleet of Ford Transit coaches whenever we needed it. Within a short space of time the company offered to supply us our own vehicle, on the same deal, which Alex accepted, willingly. No more transport worries! We were to receive a brand new bus! Seizing the opportunity, Harvey negotiated a longer-wheel-based Transit, powered by a three-litre engine, with a five-speed gearbox and overdrive. He asked for the seats to be removed and personally installed some second-hand, aircraft units with seat belts, folding trays, and reclining backs.

The next step was to tailor-make a bass 'coffin' to fit under the back row, which would cradle his valuable instrument and allow drums, amplifiers, and other paraphernalia to be stacked on it without incurring any damage.

After years of worry and discomfort we were in the lap of luxury. The band travelled together in speed and comfort, each man having his own seat and the ability to read, eat, and sleep, without aggravation to his fellow travellers. Alex took the front double bench next to Harvey, who drove, allowing him the space to stretch his limbs and accommodate his constant travelling hold-all, containing his cornet and personal bar.

This arrangement lasted for several years until Harvey eventually tired of travelling and wanted to spend more time with his family. His departure left a very large chasm needing to be filled. The answer was for Alex to employ a 'roady', (described in a later chapter). Harvey's service to the band as musician and driver was invaluable and I, personally, would like to thank him for his unforgettable contribution to the smooth running of the A W organisation

Fred Hunt and Harvey Weston

It is too late to find out much about Herbert Frederick Hunt's early days, now that he has gone and left no heirs to help me. Born in London in 1923, little is known to me of his formative years, education, or family background. I seem to remember, however, that he had several jobs, including steam presser in a laundry, apprentice coach builder, and chauffeur. Indeed, he was a very fine driver, for which the band was to become extremely grateful.

Where and how he learned to play piano I can't tell you, but I know he was involved with Mike Daniels, Cy Laurie, and Freddie Randall. He was indeed holding down the piano chair in the Randall band when Alex was invited to become the trumpeter in a breakaway outfit mentioned in another chapter. Fred adopted a good two-handed style favoured by early pioneers such as Earl Hines, Jess Stacy, and Gene Schroeder, but he was really his own master. Other influences such as Ivor Novello, Fats Waller and, to a lesser degree, Chopin and Liszt, were definable in his playing. He was a good rhythm section player as well, adapting his style to Count Basie-like economy, or Jelly Roll Morton excitement, according to the mood of the pertinent band arrangement. He was also an excellent soloist, of course, presenting his unforgettable featured solos in a style completely his own. He had the enviable ability to hold an audience's attention from the first few notes of a piece, building excitement as the opus evolved, and ending in a crescendo matched only by the cheers of his enthralled listeners.

As part of the rhythm section, I found him easy to play with. He didn't employ the use of multi-noted chords, but rather used two or three note harmonies on his left hand, leaving me to fill the spaces with fuller, passing chords, in a four-in-the-bar style, a la Freddie Greene. I feel the rhythm section was as good as any in Europe and, indeed, outside the USA, especially with Ron Rae on bass, which most of the band's overseas guests seemed to agree with.

Fred had two spells with Alex and was, in my opinion, a corner-stone in both bands. The first band, featuring the wonderful clarinettist, Archie Semple, had based its style on a mixture of Eddie Condon's Chicagoans and Louis Armstrong's All Stars. Some notable recordings are testament to the quality in this outfit and portray Fred's flexibility.

The second instalment extended his adaptability even farther. I have described already how the personnel had changed, bringing new ideas and styles with the new members. Fred fitted in like an old pair of shoes. As the tours with the American stars developed, so did his ability to accompany them and improvise solos in styles hitherto neither familiar nor associated with him. He was Schroeder, Basie, Ellington, Stacy, Powell, Hines or Morton, whenever it was required of him to add stylistic authenticity to the chosen number. But most of all he was himself. Inspired to an extent by these great pianists, Fred developed his own style and became instantly recognisable in his own right. As well as being an integral part of our great rhythm section, he produced solos of individual sound and quality such as; 'Pearls on Velvet', a medley of 'Yesterdays', and a driving "St Louis Blues', in a tribute to Earl

Hines. He even produced a wonderful version of an 'Elegy' by Jules Massenet.

Fred was extremely popular with ladies, whom, in an effort not to offend, I will describe as having probably left their best years behind them. His looks I suppose could be described as in the mould of the early stars of the silver screen. His black Brilliantine-adorned hair was trimmed in the style of Michael Rennie, and framed a craggy countenance reminiscent of Gary Cooper, Humphrey Bogart, and Gregory Peck, or a blend of all three. His teeth, his worst feature, which gave him occasional discomfort, were nicotine-stained from his excessive smoking of 'Gauloises' French cigarettes. His frame was naturally lean, bordering on sparse, and usually clothed in standard off-the-peg ware. He stood about five foot ten inches in his slippers.

He had married his first wife, Jean, when they were both quite young. By the time he re-joined the band, they had separated and Fred was sharing his life with Brenda, whom I have described in an earlier chapter. They found and rented a flat in a Kensington Mews, opposite the one occupied by Alex and which also housed Dave Lee Travis, a few doors away. With his partner, his dog Brandy, his baby grand-piano, and his boss and great mate, Alex, living opposite, Fred seemed to have found domestic bliss - except that Fred was probably one of the least domesticated musicians I ever knew.

Although familiar with the workings of the motor car, his knowledge of the functional mechanics of a washing machine or a vacuum cleaner could be described as less than basic, as was his expertise in the culinary arts. I believe he could just about boil an egg, pop some bread in a toaster, and brew a 'cuppa'. So Brenda, although working full-time, had more to do when she came home and her man was off fingering a few arpeggios somewhere. Nevertheless, the arrangement seemed to suit both of them and they appeared very contented with their new home.

Away from home, on the road, Fred made it obvious that he didn't like hotels, especially when sharing rooms, and that he missed the comforts of his home. I think this is where his female friends entered the equation. His playing seemed to reach the hearts of the ladies, who would make the effort to talk to him, husbands or partners in tow, and it would be a matter of course until he was invited to their homes for a late drink and inevitable bed for the night. As these friendships developed, the need for a hotel became less and less important. He had friends north, south, east, and west.

Brenda, of course, knew of his indiscretions, but accepted the situation. As long as she had her Fred, she turned a blind-eye to the whole business. She let slip her knowledge a couple of times by talking to her mates about Fred's 'Baggy Mauds', an apt name if ever there was one. Sometimes a lady friend would travel to see the band and stay with the pianist in the hotel. I think this is how the cat got out of the bag in the first place. A story went around that Brenda had phoned the hotel to talk to

Fred, only to be informed that her man was not available, but would she like to talk to his wife? Ouch! In the end, what did it matter if they both accepted the situation? Fred married Brenda when an appropriate occasion presented itself, and they stayed together to the end.

Indeed, I think their marriage was quite sound. Brenda had come from a West-Country middle-class upbringing and, as a beautiful young lady, had sought her fame and fortune in London. Her success as a nude pin-up model was well known. Under the pseudonym of Paula Page, she became one of George Harrison Marks' most famous and popular locker-room photographic models. A motor car accident ended this by leaving her looks slightly disfigured, by having her teeth extracted and a denture fitted. She was married to the aforementioned Douglas Gower, a car salesman, who liked jazz and, especially, the sort of jazz played by Alex's band. Brenda had had a short affair with Alex, but soon she and Fred found each other and the relationship became permanent.

Brenda had a slight air of superiority - you know the type: "done it, dearie!" Therefore, for the most part, she was disliked somewhat by the guys and their wives, with the exception of my own (first) wife, Jacquie. Their friendship eventually led to my divorce in some ways. That's another story.

If Fred ever suspected anything, he never said so and would even become excited to tell the chaps if she were coming to a gig. At home they enjoyed each other's company immensely, and one could imagine an evening of good food (Brenda was a fine cook) and wine, followed by a romantic interlude of Ivor Novello's music, with Brenda clad in the 'dining room curtains' (as one of the chaps described her evening dress), sprawled, glass in hand, over Fred's candlestick-illuminated piano. This might sound a little harsh but, believe me, they loved that idiomatic and louche style and would be delighted to be known as associated with it.

Fred had a great sense of humour and adored Laurel and Hardy. He had pictures of them on his walls and often would emit a Hardy-like "Duh!" or a Laurel-like flick of his hair when he made a silly mistake. He liked a 'taste', as did the rest of us, and could drink most of us under the table; a dubious, doubtful talent to have, although he didn't seem troubled by hangovers, weight gain, or any other side-effect associated with alcohol. He didn't enjoy or participate in sport, but was a prolific reader and film buff. His musical tastes were quite eclectic, ranging from classics, through various styles of jazz, to musicals, to Sandie Shaw, Dusty Springfield, and Kate Bush. He was a good listener and conversationalist and, of course, very knowledgeable about the Second World War, having lived through it in Blitz-hit London. I have a notion he had some connections with the Royal Air Force, but can find no confirmation of this. Above all, Fred was a charismatic, interesting, talented member of the band.

In the early 1970's plans were approved to redevelop the area around the Mews, which was to include knocking down the flats to accommodate the building of a private hospital. The couple decided to buy a house in Palmers Green, North West London, being fed up with paying rent on a property they would never own, and moving them closer to the Gowers, with whom they had remained good friends. All was fine for a while. By now they had two dogs and a nice home.

It soon became apparent to them, however, that they had taken on more than they had bargained for and started to slip into debt. I am no paragon of virtue, as the same thing has happened to me a couple of times, and therefore I can heap no blame on their backs for their desire for a better life style. Fred had heard that the place to be was South Africa. He had friends who had emigrated there and were loudly extolling the virtues of the developing country. Putting his house on the market was hard enough, but now worse was to come! He had to let Alex know of his plans and ask him to accept his resignation from the band, as soon as he had sold up. We were all upset and saddened by the situation, but could do nothing but grin and bear it.

CHAPTER TWELVE

THE BOSTON TEA PARTY

Ruby Braff was quite the shortest giant I have ever worked with, but a giant among musicians he certainly was. From his platform of early influence by Louis Armstrong, Ruby developed and advanced the art of playing jazz cornet to near perfection. His wonderful embouchure and near flawless technique enabled him to play from the quietest whisper to a roaring shout, with superlative tone and taste. In Ruby we had the master executive of a ballad, the Olympian swimmer in the mainstream of jazz, and the dictator in the Dixieland idiom.

Prior to our first tour together, my knowledge of the Massachusetts marvel was limited to a couple of records in my collection: the ten-inch Vanguard classic of the band, led by the fine trombonist, Vic Dickenson, and an album of the Jack Teagarden band. It had also been rumoured that Ruby could be, at best, difficult and at worst, downright rude, to musicians who failed to meet his high standards. Critics and ear-benders were also included in his list of those deserving a tongue-lashing. It was therefore with mixed feelings that we awaited his arrival. Although we had, with the exception of Dickie Wells, experienced no trouble with our previous guests, some of the other bands involved in tours had encountered several problems. Tenor saxophonist, Don Byas, had given Alan Elsdon an uncomfortable passage by producing an evil-looking knife on occasions, and a drunk Ben Webster had acted similarly towards gentle promoter, Bill Kinnell ('Fu' to his friends), at Nottingham's Dancing Slipper Club. Would our luck continue? We needn't have worried! After the usual introductions, we sat down to discuss the programme and Ruby produced a little pipe, which he puffed at, then passed round with the words, "Why don't you cats try a little vonce?"

He was alluding to the substance being smoked and using part of the vocabulary donated to the jazz fraternity by the late President, Lester Young; Ruby's personal version of the Boston Tea Party. Ouch!

Those with a little delectation for a turn-on (no names, no pack drill - I'm no fool!) accepted a puff, while the rest settled for a pint. But, it all helped to break the ice and ensure a relaxed rehearsal. Extricating his cornet from its leather wallet, Ruby began to play the first tune that came to his mind. One by one we joined him. As soon as it became apparent to him that we were familiar with the piece, he moved on to another. In the event of not recognising, or failure to grasp the nuances of a number, he would say, "I've always hated that one, anyway," or words to that effect.

Soon we had enough of a repertoire to draw from for the tour. Or so we thought. It's obvious now he was just sounding us out. That evening, we hardly played one song we had rehearsed. What was even more amazing was that he just began playing a tune without mentioning its title, key, or tempo; a sort of 'Spot The Tune' with A' levels! Ruby knew we could handle his approach and, with thanks to Fred's amazing repertoire and our ability to catch on, we got through the evening successfully. Ruby would adopt this formula for the rest of the tour.

One evening in the Regency Ballroom in Bath, Ruby turned to the band. "Okay, you cats, take five, just guitar!" he said.

Suddenly, feeling rather conspicuous and a trifle vulnerable, like wearing trousers made of glass, I awaited his instructions. None came! Instead, he launched straight into 'There's a Small Hotel', expecting me to know it and join him.

As it happened, I was familiar with the song, although I had never played it and I knew that the middle eight bars are a little tricky. Hearing my fumbling and, indeed, probably expecting it, Ruby turned to face me and improvised carefully round the chord structure of the tune. With a little diligence I had it! He then left me to solo on a chorus just to make sure. Fortunately, the discerning audience realised what was happening and, at the end of the number, gave us a standing ovation. I believe this was the beginning of a very happy musical relationship between Ruby and myself as, from then on, he would often play a solo in a band number to just guitar accompaniment.

He also recognised the musical ability in the front line by introducing quite demanding head arrangements that he was used to playing back in the States.

'Where's Freddie' – a tribute to guitarist Freddie Green – is one of those, captured on record on the Black Lion label, as are 'Heah Me Talkin' to Ya', and 'No One Else But You'. On one of the albums you can hear him talking, as he introduces 'Buddy Bolden's Blues'. After several tours, Ruby almost came to be regarded as one of the band members. He joined in our late night parties, even to the extent of playing piano at one impromptu session at the Brecon Hotel in Rotherham, of music, mirth, and monologues.

Rotherham is geographically well-sited for touring bands, lying in the middle of the country as it does. We had been fortunate in meeting jazz and cricket loving Athol Carr, the proprietor of the Brecon, and always stayed there. In return for a soiree with an invited paying audience in his lounge bar, we received accommodation and a small fee. This was a godsend between places such as Leicester and Kendal, for example. It was there that we discovered the wildly exciting extrovert tap dancer, Will Gaines; he was down on his luck and had been employed by Athol as a general handyman.

Ruby's famous cantankerousness rarely manifested itself on these tours and was never directed towards the band. I do, however, remember him telling a member of the press that it had been 'A great pressure meeting you!' and hearing of one unfortunate musician, best left anonymous, whom he introduced to the audience as 'A musical disease,' followed by, 'some guys miss out middle-eights, this guy misses out whole tunes!'

As his visits to London became more frequent, Ruby's friendship with Alex and his great buddy, Laurie Ridley, deepened. I think he spent a lot of his free time at Alex's flat, listening to music and chatting. All three men had great admiration for the wonderful Judy Garland; indeed, she was one of the loves of Ruby's life, his having met and befriended her at some stage.

After Alex and Laurie died, whenever I heard that he was in town, I went to see him if I could. He sometimes asked me if I had a guitar with me and I often did. On one occasion, I went to see and hear him at the Pizza Express restaurant in London.

Our own great trombonist, the late George Chisholm, whom Ruby had asked to sit in sometime, accompanied me. When George approached him he said: "No brass!" Then, turning to me, he asked if I had my guitar. Plainly shocked and upset, George took his seat while I, with a great deal of embarrassment, joined Ruby on the stage, not wanting to spoil my relationship with him. After a couple of numbers, Ruby suddenly announced: "I'd like to welcome George Chisholm to the stand!"

As ever, he did it in his own enigmatic way.

At the time of writing, Ruby doesn't visit much now. He is virtually crippled by some form of lung disorder and spends a lot of time in a wheelchair. If he never plays another note, he has left a wonderful legacy to inspire young cornettists in his many recordings, some of which I was fortunate enough to be part of.

(Since penning this, Ruby has sadly passed away, leaving the world a much less musical place.)

CHAPTER THIRTEEN

THE SINGING SINK

F or the most part nowadays, due to a combination of economics, lack of tours, and fast motorways and cars, musicians mostly perform one-night stands and, therefore, the need for overnight accommodation is largely a thing of the past. Low fees, expensive hotels, and bands no longer travelling together in one vehicle, have been the main factors.

When I joined the band in the 1960's there was no choice but to stay overnight and undertake tours, to ensure wages. With the exception of highly-prestigious, well-paid gigs that included accommodation, sometimes in the hotel we were playing in, it was necessary to shop around for the most economical digs to ensure the fee from the average club gig wasn't too decimated. Sometimes the chaps would even stay at fans' and friends' homes, and this would help matters tremendously.

These hotels were usually at the cheaper end of the market, mostly Victorian or Edwardian in construction, and pretty run down. They all boasted the same features; threadbare carpets covering creaking wooden floorboards, wallpaper peeling off damp walls, lumpy mattresses on creaky bedsprings, cold starched sheets and threadbare blankets, fading, uneven curtains that never met in the middle of the window, dark brown wardrobes with ill-fitting doors, newspaper-lined chests of drawers, and the piece de resistance, 'The Singing Sink'.

I'm no plumber, but I believe that in an effort to hygienically modernise the premises, individual sinks had probably been fitted in the rooms at different stages. I imagine old lead piping being adapted to fit the more modern, safer, copper of a different bore and connected in a snaking, uneven miasma around the edifice.

If you have ever suffered from trapped wind you will be able to imagine the metaphoric discomfort of this disjointed system, and the occasional relief it enjoyed. Imagine hot water rising from the cellar boiler, transported in inch-or-more thick pipes, forcing vents of stale trapped air into three-quarter inch tubes, filling every empty space in the system. Agonising screeches and groans would be heard from around the building, ending in a great gurgling of air and water in your bedroom sink. Not content with this, as someone emptied a bath or sink, the waste system joined in with discordant harmony, even forcing a falsetto explosion up the overflow pipe and producing an aquatic operetta, which starred as its Prima Donna, 'The Singing Sink'.

There were peak times for performances: late afternoons, when bathing was at its busiest and, of course, breakfast time, when shaving, soaping and sluicing were manifest. But prime time was when no human hand, body, or face, had any involvement, in the middle of the night. As the boiler was presumably shut down for the night and, as the water cooled and contracted, the whole operation went into reverse, causing gurgling explosions to erupt from the hand basin, followed by deep sighing as the vacuum sucked air from the room. Even plugging the drain hole had no effect as air from the adjoining room sink forced the stopper out with a plop and plunk as it hit the bowl.

Of course, musicians and other night birds were the main audience to this nocturne, having only booked into their rooms after the gig in the early hours. Usually exhausted from travelling, performing, and probably drinking too much, all that was required was a nice comfy bed in a quiet room. Ha! You must be joking! The Phantom Plumber of the Opera has other ideas!

But, somehow, even after wrestling with the spinning room (the result of over-indulgence), you drift off.

EEEEEEEE OOOOOOO WOOOOSH GAGAGA DADADA DIDIDI OOOOOH

And you are awake again.

But at least you hardly ever missed breakfast; the plumbing saw to that! And if the sink didn't get you, the vacuum cleaner outside your door did. It was actually better to nurse a hangover amid the raucous sound of clanking teacups, the clatter of cutlery, and the rustle of newspapers, than to lie in the Armageddon created by The Singing Sink.

Happy days!

I can write this with a smile now but, back then, some of the less-than-salubrious squats we were forced to spend our leisure and slumber time in, were not exactly Shangri La for us. Before I joined Alex, I had experienced some great delights, such as the Essex Hotel in Manchester, thankfully no more. It was always a Friday or Saturday evening after a gig in one of the local jazz clubs. Like so many, it had started out as a Victorian or Edwardian residence with large, high-ceilinged rooms, later converted into narrow rooms with paper-thin walls and, if you were lucky, a 'singing sink' and an in-house radio system with no choice of programmes. The sounds of snoring, farting and, of course, copulation succeeded in keeping you awake into the small hours, even after you had managed to stop the wardrobe spinning. (It was along the corridor of this splendid edifice that I witnessed Robbie Winter, our drummer, naked as the day he was born, walking on his hands whilst farting Colonel Bogey!) At breakfast the next morning you could hear guests giving the game away by asking their 'wives', "How do you take your tea/ coffee, sugar and milk?"

Even newlyweds surely know without asking!

Pianist, Bix Duff, told me of a place that the Mick Mulligan band used to stay in, above (of all things) a salami factory, which churned out the evil, garlic-fumed sausages all night long, accompanied by a regular chug-chugging from the machinery.

Mrs Mack's was another one before my experience, famous for having a photograph of Princess Elizabeth and Prince Philip, signed, 'Lovely Digs, Liz and Phil', and where Alex used to smuggle in butter for his toast.

Alan Elsdon told of arriving at a northern establishment around tea time, after a horrendous journey from Haverfordwest, and asking the landlord, "Any chance of a pot of tea?"

"Margaret! Margaret!" shouted mine host and, after the sound of hoovering ceased, "We've got a comedian here!"

Alex tried to get the best value for money and, often because of a block booking for at least seven (single rooms if you were lucky), succeeded in getting a result. But the best laid plans...gang aft agley etc, and indeed it was Scotsman, Bert Murray, who brought a happy arrangement with a hotel in

Birmingham to an end. Having a little too much to drink after one gig, Bert had caused a bit of a disturbance in his room, late into the night. Unfortunately, he had been billeted immediately above the manager's bedroom and had kept the unfortunate man and his wife awake for most of the night.

The next morning, nothing was mentioned and the band set off unaware. The next time rooms were required, Alex phoned and was told there were plenty of available rooms and was asked for the guests' names.

"Crimmins, Semple," he replied and, with bated breath, "Murray."

No response!

On being asked under whose name the booking should be reserved, and replying, "Welsh," he was asked if it was the Alex Welsh band. Alex of course replied in the affirmative, and he was immediately informed that the hotel was fully booked.

Several chapters, even books could be written on the subject, if someone could collect the anecdotes of musicians past and present and had the time and patience to record them. Perhaps someone will before it becomes too late but, then again, these incidents and stories are no doubt still happening to the current generation. I intend to end this chapter with tales of a couple which are etched in my memory.

The first time we played and stayed at Mr. Brierly's Midway Hotel near Rochester was for a Christmas function for Vitafoam. In fact, I tell a lie, we didn't stay; we drove home overnight, but not before the Master of Ceremonies jumped up on the stage after the 'Saints', and before 'Auld Lang Syne', to announce, "Ladies and Gentlemen, that's the end of the Alex Welsh Band."

Alex had used his time at the bar, when we were packing away, to befriend the owner, the aforementioned, and set up a deal for future accommodation. They had discovered a common denominator in that both Brierly and Welsh senior had been coal merchants. Over the next few years we stayed there whenever we were touring the area, and became very familiar with the staff; May, the housekeeper with the bad legs swathed in bandages and wrinkled stockings a la Nora Batty, Mrs Shepherd the doting secretary (was there an affair going on there?) and the bed chamber maid, whose name escapes me, but whose voice ("Leave your door loose!" uttered with a Manchester throaty 'r' as we went to breakfast), and her bespectacled face wreathed in horror as she entered Len's room one morning to find his 'Irish' hanging off the bedside cabinet like a dead rat! We got into a conversation with Brierly about travelling salesmen one day, and were totally horrified when he said, "Aye, we 'ad one o' them 'ere t'other day. We went through his bags, like we do, and found one of those dirty books. Well 'e 'ad to go!"

This stepping stone in the murky river of touring one-night-stands was a Godsend, but one night, towards the end of a particularly harrowing tour, it proved to be almost one step

181

too far. We were greeted at about one o'clock in the morning by a less than bright, but nonetheless accommodating night porter, who agreed, after allocating the keys to our sleeping arrangements, to provide us with a nightcap and a couple of rounds of sandwiches.

The drinks arrived and off he went to the kitchen. He returned post haste to inform us that all he had to offer was cold lamb. When we informed him that we didn't care if it was elephant's toenails, he laughed and disappeared again. After about half an hour, with seven weary blokes looking at empty glasses, he reappeared to inform us that the sandwiches were nearly prepared and to ask us if we would like another drink. I suppose someone should have noticed the freshly-bandaged finger!

The drinks arrived immediately and, after about another ten minutes, the sandwiches followed, beautifully presented on a silver salver. They were covered in blood! The poor blighter had cut himself and had run out of bread, so that he had no choice but to offer them to us. Blood sandwiches – I ask you? Seven weary chaps retired hungry, but at least had had their whistles wetted.

Another favourite was a club near Worcester, owned by a very fine ex-cornettist and his wife. We looked forward to appearing there because, with a bit of a squeeze, we could stay overnight or even a couple of days, if in the middle of a tour. John and Jill offered much more than a pail of water, and often way into the unsociable hours. Breakfast was always a delight, as was most of the food she served up but, on one particular visit, Jill surpassed herself.

"I hope you boys are hungry, I have a treat for your dinner tonight!" she informed us.

That evening, we sat down to be presented with Spam curry! I had indigestion and heartburn for three days after being persuaded to accept helping after helping of quite the greasiest food I've ever eaten.

The Halfway Hotel at Failsworth, Greater Manchester, will be forever lodged in my memory for several reasons. Bare linoleum on the bedroom floors and nylon sheets as bed linen, Roy playing with a model train set, choo-chooing to himself happily, being asked every morning if we required a fried breakfast, and beer-scented rolls in a tin box as night caps. The band stayed there for a whole week while we doubled at the local theatre, and another in nearby Eccles. After we presented our host with a pair of complimentary tickets for the show, we waited expectantly, knowing that, due to his reaction, he was no jazz lover. Three or four days later at breakfast, it came: "Fish and Chips!"

He was, of course, referring to a line from Len's 'Auf 'wiedersehn'

The wife of a shepherd, named Scott, ran a guest house in the village of my birth, Gifford in East Lothian, which we often used when in the area. One New Year's Eve, several of the guys stayed there. It was the landlady's usual habit to strip the beds and open the windows to air the rooms, while their inhabitants were at breakfast. Returning to their rooms in the hope of snuggling back into the warm nests they had not long departed, the chaps were confronted with crisp cold linen and a chilly ambient room temperature. From then on she was referred to as 'Mrs Scott of the Antarctic'.

On the whole, though, the Fawlty Towers were in the minority. Some digs were absolutely wonderful, like Bill Lambert's County Hotel at Kendal, and Atholl Carr's Brecon Hotel in Rotherham, where after-hours parties were frequent, and where we discovered tap dancer Will Gaines, who was working there as a busboy. In our time we met hotel staff who became dear friends and others best avoided.

I think the final straw came in Newcastle–on Tyne one afternoon when, for some reason or another, a hotel hadn't been reserved.   After phoning and enquiring at several establishments, we were happily welcomed at a decent looking place run by a charming Indian gentleman. As we were booking in we heard scurrying in the corridor above. On entering our rooms we found hastily made beds, still warm from their recent departed incumbents. To a man we descended the fire escape and fled in the van!

CHAPTER FOURTEEN

N.O.O.T.S

Broadcasting has always been an important medium in assisting the jazz musician in spreading the news. Whether it be the playing of recordings over the sound waves, incidental snippets used in advertising, or live television appearances, a musician or band leader never feels he has made it until he has a few broadcasts under his belt.

As a young man, I was very fortunate to be a part of a band that won a Carrol Levis Discoveries competition, with its prize of a trip to London's Playhouse Theatre to record 'Alexander's Ragtime Band' for a radio variety show.

I'll always remember the thrill of hearing myself, rough as it must have been, on our own radio, in our own house, for the first time.

Then, unlike today, when one has to scan the fine print of a programme guide with a magnifying glass to discover any jazz broadcasts at all, BBC Television and their Light Programme on the radio both carried a fair representation of the music. Of course, by 1960, there was probably too much of the wrong, inferior type of traditional jazz. Thank goodness this did not last and the media programme planners returned to a normal ratio of quality broadcasts, such as Terry Henebery's 'Jazz Club' on radio and, eventually, his 'Jazz 625' on television's BBC2. Alex's band was a regular visitor to the former and made several appearances on the latter.

The popular side of the music – the sing-along type – didn't disappear altogether though. You must remember that in the sixties and seventies, about sixty percent of broadcast music (of all styles), was either presented live or pre-recorded for a specific programme. The usual format would be a visit to a studio such as those in the complex at Maida Vale, in North-West London, to record about ten or so tunes in a three-hour session. These numbers would be inserted into a daily mixed-bag programme of music and chat, such as the 'Jimmy Young Show', at the rate of two a day, and repeated a fortnight later. For this, you received a fee for the initial broadcast, and a half again for the repeat airing. The regular bands employed were those of Kenny Ball, Acker Bilk, Terry Lightfoot, Alan Elsdon and us. In fact, at one point, we always seemed to be recording one programme or another. I think it was Roy, or perhaps John, who coined the word 'NOOTS' (Never Out of the Studios) to describe our frequent visits to Bond Street's Aeolian Hall, or the aforementioned Maida Vale. With our visits came the chance to meet lots of lovely (and some not so lovely) BBC staff members, and encounter many hilarious (and several less-than-enjoyable) experiences.

For Roy and myself, a broadcast would invariably require a trip down the M1 motorway at peak hour in the morning, to enable us to arrive at the studio ready to begin at nine-thirty. After finding a parking meter, which would have to be illegally 'fed' with coins every two hours (most meters allocated a maximum two hours, after which time, one had to find another, in a different area - b****cks to that!), grabbing a quick coffee and perhaps a light breakfast (if you had time), locating the studio and setting up, you were pretty much ready to broadcast. It then depended on who was in the production box as to whether it would be plain sailing or not.

Alex's ideal broadcast would be to arrive at the studio at the last possible moment, quickly get a sound balance and 'put the red light on'. In other words, get it recorded as soon as possible and get to the pub. Don't get me wrong! Alex knew the importance of media exposure, but he couldn't stand the dithering and bossiness of some of the sound producers and engineers. He knew (and he was right, of course), that the band, with the exception of an unintended fluffed note or other genuine musical error, always got the best result from a first take. The spark would die with constant re-balancing and re-trying for a better one! Some production teams knew this. We were always more than happy to see Royston Herbert, Barbara Page, Joe Young or Robin Sedgeley behind the control panel in the glass-fronted, sound-proofed production box. With them in charge, we knew we could be in and out! Some producers like (another) BP – a frustrated jazz musician – were nit-picking nuisances who always thought they knew better and constantly criticised the tuning or chord structure. Others were just a pain in the arse.

John Hooper and his sidekick, Freddie Harris, came into the latter category. There was absolutely no love lost between them and Alex. Hooper was an admirer of (and had produced, or been involved with, in the fifties), the Freddie Randall Band, and for some reason or other, thought of Alex as a contributor to the demise of the great trumpeter's band. Of course, it had nothing to do with Alex. Freddie was not the easiest of leaders to get along with and his musicians at the time had grown fed up with his constant bad treatment of them. They had decided that instead of leaving one by one, they would reform, with another trumpet player. Archie Semple's mate, Alex, had just arrived south from Edinburgh, and he was offered the job. Lots were drawn between Alex and Roy Crimmins as to who would lead the band, and Alex, in his own words, 'drew the short straw'. But this is 'old hat'!

Hooper, as far as Alex was concerned, seemed to 'have it in' for the trumpet-playing band leader. He was convinced that, on numerous occasions, the producer had deliberately called him Fred, without a hint of apology or redress. Hooper was one of the old-school of BBC producers, who, apart from his own personal dress sense, did everything by the book. His angular face, with its rheumy eyes and large, thin nose was always, like the rest of him, well bottle-tanned. He had thinning, dyed black hair combed straight back over his shiny weather-exposed pate. You could imagine a monocle in his right eye as he fixed his stare on you, while he drew on his cigarette, screwed into its holder. All year round he wore sleeveless, brightly coloured beach shirts, opened halfway down his scrawny brown chest, with two knobbly-boned, long arms in parenthesis. He uttered short, single syllabic sentences in a public school accent.

We could probably have taken all this without a problem if he hadn't, on top of everything else, made every session drag on to the last available minute. To assist him in his dastardly plan, he had found his perfect partner-in-crime, an ageing sound engineer by the name of Freddie Harris, a moustachioed, 'Tootal'-shirted, cravatted, school master type, who always wore a jacket made of tweed, obtained from (and tailored) on the Island that bore his surname. From the moment we entered the studio, this dithering twit would be fumbling with and adjusting the microphones. All set and ready to try a balance, we would manage about half a chorus before he would appear out of the box to fiddle with someone's microphone. On and on it went, try after try, tune after tune, while Hooper would grudgingly utter a few words of encouragement from the box such as, "We're nearly there, Fre –Alex."

After about two hours of the allotted three, the engineer would exit the control box and walk towards the piano. We all knew what he was going to do; what he should have done two hours before, if it was at all necessary. Reaching over the grand piano, he removed a cigarette packet from his pocket, and tearing a strip off it, inserted it into the back of the large flat microphone.

"That should do it!"

He did it every time we worked with him without fail. Of course it made very little difference to the sound; it was just an excuse for the time already wasted. But there was nothing we could do, so we just quietly got on with it. It was always a relief to go across the road to the Marylebone Lawn Tennis Club for a pint or two after enduring their Stadtler and Waldorf, Muppet-like performances in studio four, Maida Vale.

John Hooper did manage to get one over on Alex, however, and it was probably my lack of guile in allowing myself to be conned that led to it. The band was spending a week working in cabaret (not one of our stronger suits), at the Stockport Country Club, near Manchester. I received an unexpected phone call from Dave Shepherd, the fine Swing clarinettist, to ask if I could join his quintet for a broadcast of the type I have just described. As it was scheduled for a morning recording, I would be able to get to London by an early train, complete the broadcast, and return sometime in the afternoon in plenty of time for our cabaret appearance. The recording, which took place in the Aeolian Hall, Bond Street, went well and we finished and headed for the pub. When I entered the bar, I immediately spotted Hooper sitting in the window seat, large whisky in hand, before his afternoon production. I was quite surprised to be recognised by him, and even more so when he addressed me by name saying, "Jim! Just the chap! Look here, we're collecting for Freddie Harris who's retiring soon. I'll put you down for a couple of quid, and while I'm at it, how's about a tenner from Alex? I'm sure he won't mind!"

I handed him twelve of my hard-earned pounds, leaving me barely enough to survive the rest of the day. I was trapped and he knew that Alex couldn't and wouldn't say anything when next we worked with him. When I arrived back at Stockport and gave Alex the news, he was absolutely furious. Grudgingly reimbursing me, the angry bandleader swore he would find a way to avenge himself. I don't know if he ever did!

As I have already mentioned, Alex's approach to 'canned' broadcasting was to get the job done as quickly as possible. He believed in sacrificing perfection in sound, tone, and balance, for freshness and excitement, which often waned in run-through after run-through, and take after take. He always insisted in having the band line up as near as possible to the formation we adopted on stage, hating when drummers and vocalists had been segregated in sound-proofed cubicles he referred to as 'ice cream kiosks'. After obtaining a reasonable quality of sound he would say to the producer, "Just leave the light on and we'll do the rest!"

He was right, of course, and the more discerning of the producers and sound engineers always concurred. They knew the quality we enjoyed in the band and wanted to convey this to the listening public. Whenever a live audience was involved in the broadcast, the natural internal balance achieved by the musicians, and the adrenalin-fired excitement produced in their playing, made it easy for the production teams.

So you took it as it came, from the delights of Henebery, Herbert and Page, with their superb sound men, Sedgeley and Young, to the desperate fuddy-duddiness of Hooper and Harris. A special word should be written of 'Mighty' Joe Young, one of the better engineers, who always got a great sound from the band and who played a make-believe flute all through the recordings. Maybe he thought the band would have benefited from the extra voice, or maybe he just escaped into his own Guinness-aided fantasy. I liked him immensely.

Those days are gone, more's the pity, but I will remember them as a great experience, a source of income and enjoyment, and an important way to keep in touch with our fans. Variety is the spice of life and Alex's band had plenty of both. Television and recording studios brought different pleasures and problems to the band. Apart from 'Jazz 625', which was a programme dedicated to jazz, most television appearances by bands consisted of one, or at most two, inserts of popular jazzed-up songs in comedy and variety programmes, such as the Morecambe and Wise Show. They still appear occasionally and I am pleased to say, seem to endure the ravages of time.

Permed and picking

CHAPTER FIFTEEN

DIPSY DRIVERS

H arvey Weston's decision to leave the band brought another set of problems for which Alex had to find solutions. Harvey had been the lynch-pin; controlling the transportation of the band, organising departure times (which were totally ignored by some), seeing to the packing and doing most of the driving. He had been, as I've already mentioned, a moderate drinker – the only one in the band. I don't mean to imply that he never had a drink, or that the rest of us indulged too much but, when it came to driving, none of us was really willing to abstain enough to meet the drink-driving law and its dreaded breathalyser. It seemed the answer was to go the way of most of the other bands and hire a road manager or 'Roady' as they were commonly called. This would mean charging more in fees, and more likely taking a dip in our wages, but we decided to go ahead.

I can't recall how it came about, possibly through drummer Roger Nobes, but a chap in Luton, Pete Clarke, got the job. Short and stocky with a mop of blonde hair, Pete was well known as an amateur DJ in the town, and was always seen at jazz venues around and about. Orphaned or abandoned at an early age, he was raised by an elderly couple in a terraced house in the older part of Luton and, although he had steady relationships, he had never married and had no ties. Ideal, we thought. He was used to driving large vehicles and dealing with heavy equipment by way of his job as a tyre fitter, and carting around his heavy DJ paraphernalia.

I had known Pete for some time, as our paths had crossed at different local jazz gigs. I mentioned his father, but didn't know much about Stanley Clarke until Pete brought him to my house one day and asked if he could take on the job of mowing my front lawn. I think he craved company more than money as he virtually had to be forced to accept even enough for a pint or two. As the weeks went by, I learned a little of his past. One day I asked him about the War. Then it came out. He had been a flier in the first conflict, taking part in dogfights in Sopwith Camels and the like. I asked him if he had come across the Red Baron.

"Yes!" he replied. "But I never got him and he never got me!" Chuckling to himself, he returned to the mundane task of mowing.

Pete did the job well enough and enjoyed touring with the chaps, visiting new towns and cities and meeting our friends. Unfortunately, a couple of incidents led to his downfall. The first occurred while he was driving home from Leeds. Alex just happened to feel the bus move and looking up, caught Pete with his head back, bathing his eyes with Optrex (!) and not looking ahead at the road. The second was more final and not really his fault. We had been booked to play at the Roundhouse, the disused railway turntable in Chalk Farm, London, recently converted into an auditorium. We were part of an all-day presentation, which meant a quick turnaround between bands, with all hands to the pumps to set up instruments and the PA system. We decided to look after our own personal gear, leaving the humping and setting-up of the sound system to Pete. Our speakers were quite large – nearly as tall as Pete – and there was no back to the stage. Yes, you've got it; straight off the back he went, speaker and all. He struggled manfully on, it has to be said, but he was obviously in some distress. It turned out, of course, that he had cracked some ribs.

Alex had no choice but to lay him off. Pete graciously accepted the situation and, bearing no grudge, continued his association with the band in a mutual friendship. I frequently came across him in and around Luton in the years up to his recent, untimely death. He was still involved in jazz in the town and had learned to play bass guitar. For a little man who had a bad start to life, Pete made the most of his chances and will certainly be remembered by anyone whose path he crossed.

I think John Barnes suggested the next man for the job. Jim Fenwick, a Scot, living in Hayes, Middlesex, who was out of work, interested in jazz and considered sound and reliable by the saxophonist. Jim had a clean driving licence, experience in driving vans and a pleasant manner. Again, he wasn't a big man, unlike most roadies nowadays. He sported a short back and sides, spiky hair style, spectacles and a small, bristly moustache, but he was wiry and willing, and Alex offered him the job. He drove well and soon picked up the setting-up of the gear, although slowly and methodically at first. He wore a donkey jacket overcoat, which we soon noticed he never removed, even when perspiration was running down his cheeks. This led to his being referred to as Colombo, after the television detective.

Jim and his charming wife, Wendy, were soon welcomed in the band, even to the extent of socialising on days off. Roger Nobes, who by now held down the drum chair and his lovely wife, Sue, were frequent visitors to the Fenwick household, as were John and Pat Barnes, and my first wife, Jacquie and I.

One amusing anecdote, although I believe it happened after his term of employment, is worth repeating.

It turned out that Jim held political leanings toward the National Front movement, and this came out at an evening spent at the Barnes household. During dinner, the subject had turned to politics in general and immigration in particular, and Jim's narrow views had rankled the democratic, freethinking John. A real argument broke out, resulting in the Fenwicks' ejection. I never knew Jim held these views. He presented himself as rather a quiet, bashful sort of chap, who kept himself to himself, although I do remember his slightly more argumentative nature manifesting itself after he had partaken of a couple of beers and a drop of Scottish water. It was drink that led to his dismissal. A couple of times, we had been pulled over by the Police and the driver (although confessing to having had a couple of beers during the evening), after being breathalysed had been found to be well within the limit and allowed to go. On one occasion after Wood Green Jazz Club, however, the after-hours drinking had gone on a bit and Jim had drunk just a little too much. On the way home, he was tested and he failed. He carried on driving until his court case, but his inevitable disqualification saw an end to his job with the band. I haven't seen him in years. I hope he and Wendy are well.

So, we were back to square one.

Next up was Phil Finch, who belied his surname by appearing more like a little Cockney Sparra'. Again, diminutive in stature, he was a fine driver but found the rest of the job to be tedious. Phil was more interested in being a star than a roady and would often have to be reminded about what we paid him for. In his leisure time, he indulged in a little use of soft drugs, but drank very little, which to me were both a relief and a worry. I'll remember him for a couple of witty remarks he made regarding Fred's liking for ladies of a questionable age, especially by his standards. At one venue a septuagenarian lady met the pianist and the couple headed off to the bar.

"He's not going to do things to that, is he?" enquired the disbelieving young roady.

On a later occasion, we were driving on snow-covered roads in the middle of a nasty spell of weather. When we arrived at the gig, Phil opened the rear doors and a shovel fell out.

"That's to dig up some more stiffs for Fred!" exclaimed the driver.

Later in the evening, on spotting Fred at the bar with one his regular lady friends, who came to hear the band whenever we were in the North East, Phil was heard to say, "Cor- Blimey! He's dug annuver up!"

After Phil came George Hay, an affable young chap of joint Anglo-Germanic parentage. He liked to wear jeans and a leather jacket, which was fine by us, but   his habit of wearing sandals on sockless feet seemed a bit eccentric. He appeared to be a bit of a loner and didn't socialise much. One night in the Badewanne (bathtub) Jazz Club, in Dusseldorf, he decided to do his bit to cement good will between our nations. Firstly, as there was no need for him to drive for a couple of days, he got drunk and for a while seemed to be really having a great time but, as the beers went down, his mood changed, giving slightly more concern to the guys on the bandstand. Suddenly, beer pot in hand, he jumped onto a table just in front of us and, in a loud voice, began shouting obscenities: "Krauts! I hate fucking Krauts. Fuck off the lot of you!" or words of that sentiment.

Someone jumped off the stand and led him away, but the atmosphere that evening was difficult to regenerate, although our German friends were truly understanding and sympathetic. The next morning we discovered that he had had a hard time with his German mother, whom he had grown to dislike intensely. Alex felt we really couldn't trust him not to react again, especially as we were appearing in both divisions of Germany frequently at that time and decided to dispense with his services.

John Malone was our penultimate driver. I honestly can't remember too much about him, other than that he was quite a social animal and loved chatting, especially to landlords and pub owners, and very often after closing time. I do remember all of us, including Alex, who was often last to take his seat, sitting in the bus waiting for John on more than one occasion, while he said his farewells to the bar staff.

Alex sharing a quiet moment with Jeff Garrard.

Coming up in the rear was by far the best, most affable, longest-serving road manager (in every sense of the word) we employed.

After Len left, Alex gave the drumming job to Roger Nobes, a very good vibraphone player, who has been mentioned before, and who had enjoyed a long association with the band. Before a gig in Clacton, which was to be his audition, nobody knew he even owned drums, never mind played them. To do the gig he had persuaded Jeff, the manager of a music shop, to lend him a kit. In fairness, he did a good job, playing the right sort of two-beat rhythm required on that particular sing-along, dance gig.

A few months later, Jeff Garrard's life had hit a brickwall. As an ex drum maker for the Premier percussion company, he had risen through the ranks and become manager of the Rose Morris music shop in Shaftsbury Avenue, a good, well-paid, position, which enabled him to live comfortably with his wife, Mary, and his four children, in a semi-detached house in a good part of Dunstable. Suddenly, disaster struck! He was relieved of his job and, when spending more time at home while seeking another, he discovered that his wife was having an affair with the next-door neighbour. The poor chap didn't know where, or who, to turn to.

As it happened, we were about to fly out to East Germany and had not fixed a manager to come with us. We had always taken a sort of *general factotum* on these trips to help with baggage etc. Roger, obviously a good friend of Jeff's, suggested him to Alex; we were very pleased when the bandleader offered him the job and the unhappy fellow accepted it. The 'new boy' took to the task like a duck takes to water. His knowledge of the workings of musical instruments was beneficial, both in the setting-up and servicing of the kit and public address system. He mixed well with punters and promoters alike and understood the needs of the touring musician.

Jeff was an Englishman and proud of it. I don't mean to say he was racialist, far from it; he juFst wanted England to be English. He was born and brought up in Leicestershire (God's County, in his mind). Of average height and build, bespectacled and slightly balding, he could have passed as a bank manager, school teacher, or civil servant. As it happened, he didn't have much time for either of the first two and detested the latter with a profound hatred of their rules and red tape.

"Bloody Civil Servants!" he would exclaim, when something or someone stood in his way or held him up when driving. This led to a great event I will tell you about.

One afternoon, while heading south through London, late as usual for a pick up at the 'Hole in the Wall' pub near Waterloo station, we were stuck in traffic in Portman Street and, in particular, behind a limousine bearing CD plates. White-knuckled as he gripped the steering wheel, our driver was cursing quietly under his breath. Approaching Portman Square, the limo signalled that it was turning right towards the British Museum. Since we were going straight on, we were able to move to the inside of the shiny Bentley. As we drew level, Jeff wound down the driver's window and, leaning out, he screamed at the limousine's driver, "Fucking Civil Servant!"

The driver paid no heed, while the passenger in the back seat, HRH The Queen Mother, carried on waving serenely.

As I already stated, Jeff's home was in Dunstable, close to my own and Roy's in nearby Luton. He somehow managed, assisted by his eldest daughter (a single mother in her own right), to raise and provide for his four young children, and still hold down his job with the band, a feat to be admired. He was with the chaps for several years, becoming an honorary eighth member and combining his driving duties with running little errands for Alex as the leader's health and mobility declined.

Eventually he had enough and decided to return to Leicester, where he purchased a house to be with his growing family. He still comes to the occasional gig and I am always delighted to see him. Jeff was our final and best transport manager. As engagements dwindled and motorways were developed nationwide, there was no longer a need for such as he. Nowadays, the job for jazz bands is virtually non-existent, but our lives would have been poorer and more demanding without our own particular roadies.

Jeff Garrard telling me to keep my nose clean!

CHAPTER SIXTEEN

JAZZERS, JAZZESSES AND JOINTS

I'll start with joints. To the probable disappointment of some of you, who are expecting a revelation and confession of the widespread use of herbal cigarettes, or 'African Woodbines', among the band members, I have to tell you that you have opened the wrong book. Yes 'Mary Jane' did metaphorically associate 'herself' with some of the chaps, but in very limited appearances. I have told you about Lennie's little habit, and have to admit that I tried Mary Jane's company for a short time myself, but my association with her came to an end when, at an after-hours party in a hotel near Durham, I found myself being extricated from a wooden coat stand that I had stupidly decided to climb into, while under her influence.

No, the joints (to borrow the name from early *'jazzers'*) I am referring to here, are the pubs, halls, theatres, nightclubs, and even department stores in which we found our work.

As I have mentioned, my first gig with the band was at the Fishmongers' Arms at Wood Green, which was probably our most prolific venue in the 1960's. Although used by other bands on several evenings, our gig was on the Sunday evening, at least a couple of times a month. Too hot in the summer months, and freezing cold – to the extent of sometimes having to play in overcoats – in the winter, this wooden- floored, wooden-raftered, wooden-chaired barn, provided us with some of our happiest memories, and some of our more forgettable. The band room, piano and electrics were certainly in the latter category. So tiny you couldn't even swing a kitten in it, the space allotted for changing was freezing cold and filthy, and smelled of stale beer, fags and farts. During our time, it welcomed George Chisholm, Kenny Baker and Beryl Bryden, appearing for the home team, and Wild Bill, Bud Freeman and such, for the away side.

There was adequate space on the wooden stage (yes, more wood! - maybe that's why it was called Wood Green?) to accommodate a seven-piece band comfortably, even allowing a little soft shoe shuffle, buck and wing, or Elvis impersonation by yours truly and even a 'Crazyfoam' custard pie fight inaugurated by Barnsie, of course. Stage right, there nestled an outdated, outplayed, out of tune piano, which suffered the same seasonal temperature swings as the rest of the room, and only came back from the dead when coaxed out of its somnolence by someone like Fred.

Half way up the wall, stage left, a dangerous, inadequate, overused, two-pin 5amp socket proclaimed itself proudly as the only source of electricity available. Plugged into it were at least two or three 'adaptors' to accommodate the several units of amplification used by the visiting musicians. None of it was 'earthed'. At that time, several sizes of non-fused plugs were in use, which necessitated the user having to change his plug on every gig. An unnecessary nuisance to musicians in general and a 'pain in the arse' to me, it wouldn't be unknown to just have bared wires on the appliance rammed into the socket, and secured by used match sticks. How dangerous was that? The general use of the square peg, 13amp, system in use today was a godsend, although you still have to use adaptors and converters and such when abroad, as you know.

The audience varied little from week to week, month to month, year to year. Some, like Jonah, Jack Peacock and John Morrow, would join the band and their wives and girlfriends in the saloon bar in the main building for a pre-session tipple. Regulars would include little Geoff Watts, a dwarven trumpet player, who had suffered the added indignity of being paralysed from the waist down by a bomb explosion in the war, but who, nevertheless, turned up in his little invalid car every time, bringing his own chair-come-walking frame and finding his reserved spot near the bandstand. Occasionally Alex would hand him a microphone to give us his version of 'Georgia on my Mind', in a resonant fruity voice. Other notable regulars were 'Ma' and 'Pa' Ling and their teenage clarinettist son, Brian, who was actually featured on a short film with Freddie Randall and who now resides in Florida. Brian is a regular contributor to Facebook, where you can access the film and I talk to him often.

Also regular were bassist Buck Taylor, with his wife Rhoda, and his teen-aged, budding guitarist son, Martin. In the interval of one session, Buck approached me to ask if I would consider giving Martin a little of my time to encourage him into playing jazz. I willingly agreed and, on several Saturday mornings, they came to my home and I got him playing a few licks and taught him a few standards. He was quick on the uptake and I wasn't surprised that he improved enough in a short period to sit in with the band and eventually deputise for me on gigs, when I was indisposed. He has since become one of the world's leading jazz guitarists and received an MBE for his contribution to the genre. I hope I do not sound too proud to have been a small part in his success.

Before moving on, I would like to offer a thank you in gratitude to promoters Art and Viv Saunders, for keeping jazz going in one of the best clubs that ever existed.

London and the Home Counties offered dozens of clubs during the band's existence, too many to list here, or even for that matter remember, but I will describe a few of those where the band was popular.

Of course, top of the list was what is now known as 'the 100 Club'. In the 1950's it was the home of the traditional jazz revival led by George Webb and became the residence of the Humphrey Lyttelton band, in fact referred to as 'Humph's', even a couple of decades later by those who had been around that long. My first visit was as a seventeen-year-old on a trip to London to participate in a live radio broadcast as a prize for our young band winning the Carroll Levis Discoveries competition. I was lucky enough to be entertained by Bruce Turner's fine Jump Band. Two years were to pass before my next visit, as a new member of the Clyde Valley Stompers.

In those days, around the start of the swinging sixties, the club was unlicensed and one had to fill ones tank at the aforementioned Blue Posts before and during the performance. The open-backed, raised bandstand was situated at the top end of the cellar room, just in front of the ladies' loo. This proved to be quite a distraction to a certain young warm-blooded banjoist, as young ladies of varying shapes and sizes passed behind on their way to the amenity. Maybe that's when I started to close my eyes while playing. By the time I played there with Alex, the logo-istic '100' back board had been added, as can be seen on our album, 'Dixieland Party'. After a short, unsuccessful period, where the entire assembly was moved to the opposite wall next to the newly-erected bar, it found its permanent site half way along the long wall opposite the entrance. This also facilitated the lengthening of the bar. The building of another small bar, next to a small Chinese take-away booth at the opposite end of the room, completed the improvements, as did the introduction of tables and chairs and drapes to improve the general acoustic.

As a venue for jazz and, indeed, other genres such as R&B, the 100 Club established itself as one of the leading three, together with the Marquee Club and, of course, Ronnie Scott's. As such, it attracted all the main bands and international stars, from the three B's (Barber, Bilk and Ball), legends like George Lewis and the Rolling Stones. During the 'trad boom', bands appeared there seven nights a week and the place was heaving. Alex's band became a favourite in its own right and by accompanying visiting Americans on tour. The 100 Club became a haven for musicians to meet and often drink into the early hours and everyone probably has at least one favourite story of a visit there. I am sure there is an unwritten book about the 100 Club and one can perhaps hope that its owner, Roger Horton, might find time to write one in his retirement.

As already stated, there were, of course, many, many pub/clubs in and around London, too many to list here, but all playing their part in keeping jazz alive in the capital.

Each club had established its own unique character and characters. Ken Lindsay and his colleagues, who ran the Hertfordshire Jazz Society and the Red Lion at Hatfield, (where I introduced myself to my hero, Barney Kessel, saying my name was Jim Douglas and hearing him answer an unbelievable, "Yes, I know"); ex-tax inspector, Steve Duman and his fine clubs in Morden and Pinner (where Alex met Maggie) (and I instantly regretted being married); The Thames Hotel at Hampton Court, The Salisbury Arms at Barnet, the Black Prince Hotel at Bexley and Osterley Rugby Club, with Uncle Charlie's hot dogs, all bring back happy memories and renewed acquaintanceships on each visit.

There were, of course, fans (for want of a better word), who turned up at several of these: the late Bill Morgan and his cricket and jazz-loving son, Nick, who umpired and batted respectively for the matches that we played for charity against Jimmy Greaves' team; Eddie and Marie, Bill Bailey and his wife Marian, Hugh Yorke-Barber (known to us as 'New York Harbour'), who occasionally sat in on drums – the list goes on. Please forgive me if I decline turning this into a 'who's who' of Alex Welsh Band Alumni, but those of you I have missed, please be assured you all played such an important part and will always be in my memory.

The same situation repeated itself all over the country and, indeed, Europe. Liverpool, Manchester, Birmingham, Nottingham, Derby, Bristol, Bath, Sheffield – the list is endless

– and in every town, city club, or concert hall, familiar faces welcomed us. You know who you were and are; my personal thanks to all of you.

Of course, everywhere clubs had their own regular (usually semi-professional) bands, who, week after week, month after month, kept jazz alive; unsung heroes, all of them. Again there were too many to list, but Mick Shore, Les Bull, and Johnnie Johnstone stick in my memory as having had fine bands.

Apart from the tours with visiting Americans, we were often graced with the presence of guests, such as Humph, George Chisholm, Bruce Turner, Beryl Bryden, etc. In the 1970s, directly as a result of successful concerts at the South Bank Complex in London, organised by Michael Webber (some of which were recorded and are still available from certain sources on the internet), a concert tour called 'Salute to Satchmo', involving the band and the former three aforementioned guests, played the length and breadth of the country to great success.

One of the more unusual venues the band played on a regular basis was Coombe Haven Caravan Park and Entertainments Centre, near Bexhill-on-Sea. The owner, drummer David Kenny, had a story to tell in his own right. David had first entered the jazz scene as a roadie for the great Joe Daniels and, through a series of business ventures, including selling silk scarves, had come to caravans to make his fortune. Starting with a couple and rocketing to thousands, Gailey Caravans had an overnight success with the sale and rental of mobile homes.

Somewhere along the line, Dave, as we knew him, had met and married his diminutive wife, Yvonne, who had been the bassist with the all-girl Ivy Benson Band. They set up the site at Bexhill with a large complex of auditorium-cum-dance hall, a small lounge, two nice bars and toilet and laundry facilities next to the caravan site. He then decided to present entertainment from all sides of the business, including jazz bands such as Kenny Ball and ourselves, sometimes with guests like Anne Shelton and even Maynard Ferguson. It was Hell! Can you imagine trying to play in a large echoing room on a high stage with the constant noise of children shouting and screaming, and even running across the stage? You've got the picture.

To make matters worse, or better, depending on how you saw it, Dave's generosity was legend. Not so much in the fees, which were obviously adequate, but in his stand at the bar. As soon as he arrived, you were invited to partake of gentlemen's measures, so, by the time you took the stand, you could already be 'three sheets to the wind'. Sometimes we were booked to play in the small lounge and that was great, but Death Valley, no thanks! We called it Doom Haven.

David didn't just turn up there; he often made an appearance at clubs and concerts, and even put on functions at places like the London Hilton, where he would entertain his friends from other walks of life, such as racing driver, Graham Hill and magician, David Nixon. He discovered Southern Comfort liqueur, a whole bottle of which he would pour into an ice-filled pewter tankard and pass around. I was so sorry to hear of his passing. My friend, bassist Ron Russell, is still in touch with his family and we reminisce often of the great times we had with him.

As a fitting finale to my rambling reminiscences, I must mention the wonderful Island of Jersey. What started as a 'Special Jazz Train' from Paddington to Swindon, culminating in a concert in Bill Reid's nightclub, before returning to London, blossomed from the brainwave of British Rail advertising executive, Bill Collier, to become a weekend trip to St Helier, organised in conjunction with the late Sir Billy Butlin.

Overnight by train and ferry, band, wives, fans and families descended on Portelet Bay Holiday Camp, just before the season started, giving its staff a dress rehearsal. What ensued over the weekend and for several years after will stand high on my list as some of the most enjoyable experiences in my time with the band. Sharing the stand with a band of local musicians, surrounded by a captive audience of friends and jazz lovers, who had braved sea sickness and hangovers to be there, and being treated to great hospitality by the camp staff (no pun intended), the band produced some of the best performances I can remember. Wonderful!

Humph and Chiz

Other wonderful memories include our appearances at Antibes (where the announcer told our audience our first number was to be 'I Got Rid of Them') and Nice (where I met Pee Wee Erwin and Johnnie Mince, and was complimented on my playing by another hero, Red Mitchell and where I saw Harry Edison kick off on an ethnic-based rant, oblivious to our being in the same coach) and our adventure in Scapa Flow to play for oil workers, where a middle-aged, toothless, cleaner made a fortune as the Gobbling Granny and where you couldn't move in the room at the end of the performance for empty beer cans stacked to the ceiling! So there you are. Jazzers, Jazzesses and Joints, or perhaps Heroes, Heroines and Heaven. You were to me.

As a footnote to this chapter, regarding my friendship with football manager Bill Dodgin and my being a Manchester United fanatic, I must tell you of the occasion he arranged for me to visit Old Trafford as Fulham Scout. On picking up my ticket at the office, I was amazed to read 'Admit One, Visiting Directors' Box'. Man Utd were playing Leicester City. Taking a back seat in the box I quietly, intently, watched the match. The inevitable happened, as my hero, Denis Law, scored. Completely forgetting my environment, I leapt to my feet and, arms raised, let out a yell of delight, much to the bewilderment of the Leicester contingent in the box. My embarrassment was fortunately momentary and, after the match, I had the great experience of having a drink in the bar with some of my heroes.

CHAPTER SEVENTEEN

CURTAIN UP...AND DOWN

By the early seventies, several British jazz bands had successfully ventured behind the so-called Iron Curtain, between Eastern and Western Europe, to undertake concert tours of Russian satellite countries, such as Poland, Czechoslovakia and, the most strictly controlled of all, the Deutsches Demokratische Republik, or DDR, as it was known. (In the West, it was known by the more familiar letters, GDR {German Democratic Republic} or simply East Germany.) For reasons best suited to this narrative, which will reveal themselves at a later stage, I intend to refer to it from now on as the 'DDR'.

The deal for the musicians was an unusual one. At enormous costs to the organisers, a large percentage of their annual foreign money entertainment budget was offered to the artists. Together with an extraordinary amount of East German Deutschmarks, we were paid a small amount of £sterling in return for a two or three-week tour of their major towns and cities. (In fact, the sterling part of the deal was just about sufficient to keep things going at home while we were away.) The Deutschmarks, on the other hand, gave us almost millionaire status in a country, which, to put it euphemistically, frowned upon capitalism, especially of that order. The drawback, of course, was the inability to exchange the money, or indeed to even take it out of the DDR.

The money was paid to Alex in instalments, neatly tied up in brown paper wrappers, each consisting of several thousand marks. The first evening we arrived on the very first tour, we had received a one hundred mark banknote to keep us going. Even this nominal amount seemed to be a fortune, but nothing was to prepare me for the shock of my taking delivery, as the temporary band cashier, of the first package. I remember we were in Dresden that evening, and I was handed the loot just as we alighted from the coach at our hotel. If my memory serves me well, I believe I was sharing twin accommodation with Roy, and it was with growing excitement that we opened the package in the privacy of our room. Then I knew how bank robbers or lottery winners must feel. There in front of our incredulous eyes, were literally thousands of marks in neat bundles. Apart from when possibly playing Monopoly, or some such board game, I don't think either of us had ever beheld such tangible riches. The temptation was too much! Grabbing a bundle each, we tore off the wrappers and threw the notes high towards the ceiling, laughing hysterically as they descended like snow upon our heads to land all over the room. But good sense prevailed and we picked up every last note and carefully returned it to its bundle.

That night, two contented musicians went readily to sleep in the knowledge of their new-found, fool's-paradisiacal wealth. The next morning I carefully counted out each musician's share; a personal small fortune by the standards we were used to back home. When we were on the coach and setting off to the next destination on our itinerary, I passed among the chaps, handing them their first instalments.

"What's this?" enquired Fred, who had been the last on the coach, keeping us waiting a few minutes. "Surely you've given us too much?"

"Just you be quiet!" I replied, "And what's more, anyone who's late tomorrow will get paid twice!"

As the tour progressed we accrued more and more money, and although living like kings, never seemed to spend any of it. We bought dinner, of course, and champagne in the hotel night bars, but the wad of notes in our pockets seemed to grow, rather than diminish. But back to the first tour!

After a good night's sleep and a hearty breakfast, we were introduced to two of the nicest people I have ever come across in my many travels. They were our driver, Wolfgang, and tour manager/compere, Karl Heinz Drechsel. If I ever knew Wolfgang's surname, I'm afraid it has long since disappeared from my memory, but his face and extraordinary personality will forever be etched on my mind. He stood around six feet tall, with a broad chest and brawny forearms, which burst out of his rolled-up shirt sleeves. His handshake was strong and firm. A weathered countenance was adorned by a shock of nearly white hair, sticking skywards in defiance of gravity. His face wore a continual gap-toothed smile and his eyes danced with mischief.

"Hello!" was his first utterance, followed by, "Take it easy, no hurry, in this country we have many moments!"

His voice was deep and guttural, with a heavy Germanic accent, but his command of English was good and of great help to his non-German-speaking passengers. Wolfgang worked like a Trojan, whether driving hundreds of kilometres on autobahns pockmarked by use and un-repaired since the war, or fetching and carrying musical instruments, drinks, and other errands for his more than grateful recipients. He wouldn't touch a drop of alcohol before the coach was secured for the night and, even then, it was limited to two or three quickly-swallowed bottles of beer to wash down his supper from the banquet, which always awaited us back at the hotel. His sense of humour bordered on the practical joke type, without any harm or too much discomfort to his target; he found Lennie Hastings hilarious. One by one we all experienced his sense of mischief.

My turn came one morning in Berlin. Driving along past the Russian barracks, we stopped suddenly outside an impressive old building. Alighting from the bus, he approached a young lady walking by and, after talking to her for a few minutes, called me out of the coach. Slipping the girl's arm through mine, he positioned us in front of the building and took a photograph of us.

"What was all that about?" I asked when we had moved off again.

"The lady doesn't like it here, so now she comes to England with you!" was his reply. "That building was the Heiraten Bureau for people to get married, and now she can say her husband is British!" Laughing at the top of his voice, he drove on.

Wolfgang drove for us on several tours, during which time he became a very good friend to all of us. One day we arrived at the airport and someone else was waiting. No Wolfgang. Things wouldn't be the same. But, in fact, things had improved for him. He had earned a reputation of trust and reliability with his State employers, and had been entrusted with the job of ferrying West German visitors along the 'no man's land' of the Unter den Linden, between the sectors of Berlin; a high honour indeed. From time to time, he appeared at our venues or hotels for a chat and a beer, but I haven't seen or heard of him since the Wall came down. Maybe I'll make some enquiries. I do hope he is safe and well.

Karl Heinz Drechsel was and still is one of Germany's leading authorities in jazz. Married with two sons, he lived in an apartment in Berlin, the walls of which were lined with hundreds of jazz albums, which he had largely received as gifts from visiting musicians from all over the world. A compassionate man of medium stature, slightly receding in the hairline, he had a soft smile and soulful eyes that quite often appeared tear-filled as he recalled acquaintances, or stories, or when one of the chaps treated him to a meal or gift. He was obviously the top man in his job as radio announcer and raconteur. As a concert compere, he was second to none.

His job with us was to be our constant interpreter and trouble-shooter, as well as introducing us to local dignitaries and VIPs and making the opening introductions at the concerts. The latter he did with great assuredness and fluency. He had obviously done his homework on all of us individually, as well as collectively as a band. But his biggest talent was observation. Each day he watched and listened to our jokes and nonsense and noted our likes and dislikes, interests and hobbies. Each evening his introductory speech got longer and longer and we would hear and recognise our names in his orations. Then it dawned! He was telling the audience of our escapades on the tour, painting a word picture of us, if you like and, in the meantime, breaking down any barriers that may have existed between our audiences and ourselves. As it happened, there were no barriers anyway. I personally found the people I met to be knowledgeable, warm and friendly.

Without jeopardising his career or obvious position of trust, he enlightened us about the way things were in the Soviet-run country; although freedom of movement from east to west was forbidden and the fripperies of capitalism non-existent, the basics of life were of a reasonable quality. Accommodation was sound and warm, clothes, although not of the latest fashion, were well-made and durable and food and drink stable, if not plentiful in variety. Shops, much as in the West today, offered the same fare wherever one went, with products only manufactured locally or in other Soviet Republic satellite countries, solely available. At the higher end of the scale this included photographic equipment from Carl Zeiss of Jena (binoculars, cameras lenses and such), and a huge range of classical music in the form of well-produced LPs and sheet music.

To augment a relatively small population, young people were encouraged to marry early and, hopefully, to produce many offspring. I have a theory that this backfired somewhat, as there seemed to be many young, single women, left with a child after an early separation or divorce. Many of the young men were, of course, serving in the Army where, I suppose, the temptation of greener pastures was omnipresent. Everyone had a job of work to do, which had led to the foundation of perhaps the most successful kindergarten system in the world, run, of course, by totally professional people.

In every city or town we visited, the opportunity to befriend a lady was presented to us in the hotel night bars where, after purchasing a bottle of bubbly, one would find oneself in the company of several local lovelies, glad to share a glass. This was not in any way prostitution; money was never a topic in any discussion, or a consideration in any relationship formed. Musicians, artists, and jazz buffs were always present too, hoping perhaps to hear a tale or two about their favourites. All of them were well-mannered, educated, interesting people, who tried extremely hard to converse with us in a language learned from films and various forms of the media, there being no English taught in schools and their second language being of course, Russian.

On the last tour the band made, I had just come through an unhappy divorce from my first wife and, I'm afraid to say, availed myself of the situation avariciously. But every one of these ladies meant something to me. I was just as glad of their warmth and friendship as I think they were of mine. At the time, Alex was married to the lady who, years later, after his sad passing, became my wife, as many of you will know. Maggie had witnessed my escapades, but never uttered a word of criticism at the time, or mentioned them in the years that followed, other than in some lighthearted reference. The night the Wall came down, we were sitting watching events unfold on the television. Suddenly a voice to my left said, "I hope this doesn't mean dozens of East German women on our front doorstep, waving paternity orders!"

I am glad to say this situation never arose, but I am eternally grateful to her for her understanding and sense of humour.

My first impressions of the DDR were of sadness and disbelief at what little change had taken place since the War. Our first port of call was, indeed, the city of Berlin or, rather, the largest part of it, which was enclosed, of course, behind the Wall. Sombre grey buildings, beautiful in their glorious architecture, still showed the pockmarks and strafing of Allied bombing and gunfire. Street lighting and paintwork was dim and drab, and a heavy atmosphere hung over the city once renowned for its gay night life. Ancient tramcars and trolley buses chugged along among the small, smelly Trabant cars, on wide streets and boulevards less than busy by today's Western standards. People hurried along, heads down, about their business, clad in colourless, durable, unfashionable clothing and, everywhere, police, soldiers, (German and Russian) and other uniformed officials were conspicuous by their numbers. The smell of cheap Russian and Baltic tobacco pervaded the air in every building, hotel and cafeteria, sometimes effusing with the acrid aroma of machine gun oil from the weapons cradled by the guards.

New buildings had, of course, been erected since the War. They consisted mostly of high-rise apartments and skyscraper hotels, or business blocks. Hotels boasted modern-style interiors, with large reception areas close to surreptitiously-supervised elevators, which led to adequately-furnished en-suite bedrooms, with double-glazed windows and double beds, television and telephone facilities. In all of them, I had a feeling of being watched or, at least, overheard, although this was probably an association of ideas, formed by reading too many spy thrillers in my youth.

Restaurants were smart and expensive, offering a selection of wares not available in the shops. Although there was usually plenty of room, large queues of local residents and businessmen were often waiting to be seated, while we and other visitors to the country were swept immediately to a table. Sundays saw the tables jam-packed with West Germans on a one-day pass to either visit relatives or simply as tourist diners, much to the annoyance of the obviously embittered waiters, who had to serve their more fortunate, free-living fellow countrymen.

But, when it came to culture in the form of music and the arts, together with their attitude to sport, the DDR were world leaders. Everywhere we performed, we had full houses in huge auditoriums, theatres and concert halls, beautifully decorated with comfortable seating for the audiences, these edifices being state-of-the-art. Backstage was no exception: large, comfortable dressing rooms, with full toilet amenities. A range of drinks and other, more substantial, refreshments relaxed the artist before and during a performance. Fireman zealously guarded buckets of fire-quenching sand and other extinguishers. Much-frowned-upon smokers had a small designated area to satisfy their craving, always monitored by one of the aforementioned pyre-technicians. Everywhere, there were huge signs, celebrating the success of the first thirty years of the New Republic ('30 jahre DDR'), with great logos of the letters 'DDR' emblazoned on them.

"Now I know why they call it the DDR!" remarked Fred Hunt, a dedicated user of nicotine, one day. "It stands for thirty years of 'Don't Dare Rauch! '"(No smoking, to you and me.)

As I intimated, concerts, for the most part, were extremely well attended – mostly sold out, in fact – by a curious audience, eager to hear a musical medium still in its infancy or, at least, childhood, in their classical music-orientated country. What surprised and astonished me was the manner in which they came and left the auditorium. One minute there would be only staff and performers, the next the place would be packed. Exactly the reverse situation occurred at the close of the performance, there being a packed hall one minute and, ten or so minutes later, empty car parks, roads, streets, and pathways. I suppose analysts would put it down to 'conditioning', but it was nevertheless a bit eerie and strange to we performers, who were more used to members of the audience staying around for a chat at the end of the concert.

During the performance, the audience went wild with enthusiasm, clapping solos and, at the close of a particular favourite number, calling for an encore by a prolonged single, rhythmic clap, which would break into wild applause when Alex complied with their request. In 1971, we were asked if we would agree to a recording of one of the concert performances, to be issued as an LP album for the Amiga label. Alex agreed and the Dresden Hygiene Museum was chosen as the venue. Although there was a blazing row going on between Alex and Roy concerning the microphone level all through the first half, what was originally issued as a single album in the DDR and, later as a double on Alan Bates' Black Lion label, turned out to be one of the best performances that the band ever recorded. It is still popular thirty years on and can be purchased as a CD on the Candid label. It was little surprise to me that the recording was good; being accepted and treated by the audiences the way we were, led to inspirational playing by the chaps.

At the close of every performance, after the mandatory ego-boosting encore, one or two lovely German lassies would appear from the wings, arms filled with bouquets of flowers, which they presented to us individually, as they might to a diva at an opera. As we were usually moving on the next day, these flowers were often redistributed to someone who had caught our eyes during the performance, to the obvious delight of the recipient.

When the adrenalin had subsided and we were all packed up, we returned to the hotel for a quiet nightcap, but other people had different ideas! Invariably a reception would await us; local dignitaries, promoters and such, saw to it that the evening didn't quite end there and would have organised what can simply be described as a banquet. Sometimes it would be a selection of cold foods, at other times a warm buffet, but there was always something to be washed down with copious quantities of wine or beer, while, all the time, hilarious discussions between non-German-speaking Englishmen and their non-English-speaking German counterparts developed with great seriousness and lack of embarrassment on the parts of the perpetrators.

This leads naturally to a situation that arose in our hotel lobby in the same city of Dresden one afternoon, while waiting for Wolfgang to arrive. Fred Hunt had brought his wife Brenda; a well-meaning but 'seen-it-all, done-it-all, and got the tee shirt' person, who could sometimes also appear to be a little pretentious. The only English newspaper available in the DDR was the 'Morning Star', which was contrary to her political style and she therefore resorted to reading a French equivalent publication. I don't know how good her grasp was of French, but she obviously had some inkling of the language. Anyway, that particular afternoon, John Barnes was seen talking heatedly to a Russian soldier. If you remember the 1970s, and the fashionable 'wet look', you will realise what I mean when I say that John looked more like a Russian than the Russian native. Attired in a shiny, calf-length, wet-look overcoat, with an Astrakhan collar, calf-length boots, and a simulated fur hat, with his jutting, bearded jaw, he looked for all the world like a latter-day Lenin.

On approaching the couple, English names such as Bobby Charlton, Denis Law and George Best could be heard being uttered from both sides. (They were obviously discussing the Manchester United football team, needless to say.) Somebody remarked, "What are they talking about?"

"You don't expect me to speak English, French, and Russian, do you?" enquired a supercilious Mrs Hunt.

The next day I caught her reading the latest edition of the French publication and, always eager to glean the latest news from home, I asked her for any information she had acquired from her readings. Not realising that my French, although by no means fluent, was a good deal better than hers, or that, having already perused the headlines, I was setting her up, she informed me what was going on in the Western world. It's quite astonishing how people translate simple news coverage in such diverse ways!

As the tour progressed, we accumulated more and more money, with no time to spend it, and very little to buy, if we had. All the time, Karl kept reassuring us that we would be able to buy everything we dreamt of when we reached Leipzig towards the end of the tour, and we would have a whole day to do it. The great day duly arrived and, after breakfast, we set out in diverse groups. Karl, of course, was right. The Centrum stores, if not laden, were adequately stocked for our needs: watches, cameras, binoculars, records, music, sporting equipment, leather luggage and even clothes were widely available to us temporary millionaires. Everyone had a field day, with one exception: Lennie Hastings, who had decided to go back to bed for an hour or so after breakfast. We were all sitting around in the hotel lounge, listening to a string quartet and discussing our bounty when suddenly Karl Heinz sprang to his feet. He had spotted a wig-less, tee-shirted, bleary-eyed drummer, descending the staircase to the foyer.

"No! No! Lennie! You mustn't appear in your undervair!" he almost screamed in horror at the apparition.

With a few well-chosen curses under his breath, the reluctant hero returned briefly to his room to return more suitably attired and wearing the famous toupee. He had, if I remember correctly, about an hour to spend his money. Somehow he managed it with time to spare. But what had he bought? Well, I can't be totally accurate after all these years, but I do remember at least half a dozen plastic suitcases and holdalls, a couple of reasonable watches, and several other useful acquisitions, but the best was to come.

"You should see what I managed to get for Jan!" he exclaimed, and held up a clock in the shape of Big Ben and the Houses of Parliament, with the German equivalent of *a present from Leipzig* written on it. Only Lennie, in the whole world, would have spotted that one.

When we checked the baggage in at the departure desk at the airport, we had over four times the number of items we had arrived with, including skis, bedding and a French horn. Excess baggage costs were paid for by the agent without a murmur on his part. What East German money we had left we donated secretly to a tearful Karl and a brave-faced Wolfgang. And so we ended a typical visit to East Germany. My lasting impressions are of the mixture of decay and flashy splendour (such as the twenty-foot high bust of Karl Marx in the city originally known as Chemnitz, then named after the founder of Communism), the poverty of the masses in contrast to the opulence of the State uniforms, the resignation on the peoples' faces to the fact that they would never be allowed to leave their country and the obvious lack of any form of crime.

Over the next decade or so, I visited the DDR nine times with different organisations. On every single occasion I was treated with friendship, dignity and respect. I enjoyed every minute of every occasion, whether brushing soot-covered snow off the window sills in Zwickau, staring in awe at Colditz Castle, or marvelling at Fred Hunt playing Franz Liszt's actual piano in his house, in the beautiful republic of Weimar. It would take a book in its own right to describe the grandeur of the Prussian Palace of Sans Souci, in Potsdam, where we also visited Cecilienhof, the site of the signing of the treaty which ended the war; the ruins of the Palace in Dresden, the Cathedral in Erfurt in all its isolation, and Johann Sebastian Bach's Leipzig heritage.

To witness what is left of the memory of the Holocaust at the camp at Buchenwald, is almost too painful to anecdote, but that I must, because I did see it, in all its horror and will never forget the feeling of despair that hangs over it. Most of all, I will never forget the East German people. Now that the Wall is no more, and Germany is in the process of reunification, I hope every single one of them can adapt to the Western ways and in doing so I pray they find everlasting happiness.

CHAPTER EIGHTEEN

RIDDLE THE YIDDLE

I t is unlikely that anyone has written or, indeed, will write about the honorary ninth member of the band: Alex's best friend, Laurie Ridley.

This schmutter merchant, would-be vaudeville entertainer, aspiring nightclub owner, opera lover, money lender, frustrated guitarist, immaculate, extrovert dresser, first-class host and entertainer, a literate and, most of all, wonderful human being, is on my short list of the greatest people I have ever known. Add to those attributes, jazz buff, Marx Brothers authoritarian and impersonator, fellow author, and Gerald Kersh fanatic, and you may just about begin to realise why we all loved this complex, unfulfilled character.

I have to confess that I didn't take to him immediately. On our first meeting at the Cottage Club, I found him garish, loud and know-it-all. His hair was just too polished, as were his expensive gold watch, his diamond stickpin and his hand-made leather shoes. The jacket of his tight-fitting Italian suit was unbuttoned to reveal an embroidered waistcoat over a dazzling white shirt, with its starched collar and cuffs fastened by glistening links. In his lapel he wore a floral buttonhole and his right hand held a gold-mounted ebony cigarette holder, containing an un-tipped cigarette.

He lived in the same opulent style in a basement flat in an art deco block in Shepherd's Bush, West London, and drove a gleaming British-racing-green, 2.8-litre Jaguar motorcar. When he spoke, his accent was North London Jewish, and his sentences were freely punctuated with Yiddish words such as schmuck, schlemiel, schnorrer, etc. He believed that the biggest insult you could give to anyone was to call him or her what they were in the nature of their employment. For example, "You, you're nothing but a tailor."

Whether slightly dyslexic or perhaps possessing a hereditary trait, Laurie had trouble pronouncing certain words. A hundred thousand, for instance, always came out as "humbert grand". Especially when discussing fiscal matters, he always referred to the lower denomination was by their

Cockney equivalents; a monkey, a pony, etc. When I knew him better, this became an endearing trait but, at first, it annoyed me intensely.

His tipple was brandy or, rather, good cognac, which he consumed in 'Gentlemen's measures', expecting his fellow imbibers to accept the same quantity when he was 'in the chair'.

The first impression (after immediate dislike) he made on me was that he was putting on an act, desperately trying to appear a character. In truth, I think he was. Just like his bosom buddy, Alex, I don't think anyone really got to know his true, innermost self.

After a few months, my feelings towards him mellowed somewhat. His generosity appeared to be genuine, as did his love for jazz in general and Alex's band, in particular. One thing still puzzled me, however. Whenever I had the occasion to travel in the back of his car, I found myself completely ignored while Alex and he discussed matters (usually women) in muted tones in the front. One evening, on our return to West London from the Fishmonger's Arms, I bearded the lion in his den by asking them why they shut me out. Perhaps paranoia had set in, but I just blew my top and told them that, although I appreciated being in the band and the offer of a lift, it would also be nice to be accepted as a friend, over and above. I was never ignored again. Indeed, I recall a visit to agent and writer, Jim Godbolt's apartment, listening to records and going up in their estimations by my knowledge of, and ability to recognise, musicians they obviously thought I was too young to have even heard of.

In 1964, Laurie was partially responsible through his connections for arranging a working holiday for the band members and their wives. We were to cruise the Mediterranean Sea on board a P&O luxury liner, the SS Iberia, for ten days or thereabouts. In return for First Class passage, we would play for dancing for an hour or so every other day. Realising we would require dinner jackets to wear in the dining rooms and a small sum of spending money for socialising, Laurie supplied both. I managed to save the princely sum of fourteen pounds, which at the time would probably have been sufficient, but I never seemed to spend anything. Every time I went to buy a round of drinks Laurie got in first, and not just me, in case you are thinking my Scottish canniness was foremost in my mind; all the chaps got the same treatment. I shared a cabin with him and wanted for nothing. When we went ashore in Athens, or some such romantic port, we pooled some money as a party and I always seemed to get back too much change. That was Laurie's way. I realised then, for the first time, I think, that, contrary to my theory that he was buying friendship, he just simply adored entertaining and gained enormous pleasure from giving.

A second slightly longer cruise, visiting several new-to-us ports of call, followed the first. On the whole, this was a tragic adventure in several ways. Firstly, there was wife trouble. Alex and Carol (his partner at the time), were not hitting it off at all.

She decided she had had enough and decided to fly home from the next place of visit, Malta. With her would go a reluctant Jan Hastings, who had received a *cri du coeur* from her baby-sitting mother, who had gone down with 'flu.

While on the island, it had been arranged to film a television special of the band, which I have unfortunately never seen and which is now probably non-existent. Back on board everything started to settle down. Ron Mathewson had bought an eight-millimetre film camera and was filming everything, fortunately using his good eye. And, there was to be a fancy dress evening. Laurie was magnificently dressed as Charlie Chaplin and won a prize, but he wasn't finished! After Ron had captured 'Charlie' on celluloid, Laurie disappeared. We were all relaxing round the pool when suddenly, faintly at first, we heard the sound of an old-fashioned bulbous car hooter. It grew nearer. Suddenly, round the bulkhead, appeared 'Harpo Marx'. Continuously hooting and cavorting, the redheaded clown made several circuits of the pool and with a splash, ended in the middle of the water, while the band and other guests held their sides with laughter. It was Laurie, of course. Somewhere there may exist a very old, well-shown film of all this, probably at Ron's home. I do hope so.

The cruise was to end on a sad note, however. Because of bad weather, we couldn't dock at one of the Greek islands scheduled and, late the same evening, the Chief of Staff, a very nice man called Graham Whitehouse, disappeared overboard, while battening the hatches. Several rumours flew around about his death as to it being accidental or otherwise. It was none of my business then, and it still isn't.

Laurie was the younger son of Harry Posner, who, after breaking away from the London firm, famous for fabrics and drapery, had changed his name to Ridley and entered the world of boxing and bookmaking. Laurie's brother, Stanley and sister Gloria, had kept faith with their roots, while Laurie followed his father and his adopted identity. I believe with some degree of acrimony, young Lawrence had also severed his ties to the family business and set up his own *Maison Ridley.* He had acquired a suitable property in Eastcote, Middlesex and opened his doors for business. Obviously unable to make a living by merely selling locally, Laurie had set up a successful mail order business.

As a young man it seems Laurie had not seen his future in the rag trade and had trodden the boards in variety shows with his good friend, accordion player and jewellery manufacturer, Jack Pritchard, and I believe this was where his heart lay. Like jazz appears to have today, variety had outstayed its welcome by the 1960's, and he had long since given up any hope of success in that field when I first met him. He still amused himself and those closest to him by writing after-dinner speeches, comic articles and poetry, of which he had had several stanzas published. Until the day he died, he held aspirations of owning his own nightclub, 'Laurie's Dixieland', featuring the best of that particular form of entertainment.

As I mentioned, Laurie played guitar. He owned a 1950's' Grimshaw Plectric, which had a lovely fingerboard, but a disappointing natural acoustic tone, which annoyed him intensely. In later years, whenever I visited his home, the guitars would come out of their cases and a jam session would follow. As the brandy went down and the session warmed up through Limehouse Blues, Avalon, and other standards, Laurie would get more and more excited, eventually bursting into song in a frantic version of the old Vaudeville song, Miserlou.

With the exception of the two cruises he co-organised and a visit to Scotland, which I intend to describe in detail later, Laurie hardly ever set foot outside London. The Fish, The 100 Club, and the Thames Hotel at Hampton Court, were his most regular gigs. Immaculate as ever, even in the damp sweaty atmosphere of the run-down pub rooms frequented by a large percentage of anoraks and sweaters, Laurie would jive the night away. He was a very good dancer, especially proficient at the Jive and Charleston. Occasionally Alex's girlfriend, later his wife (and indeed, now my own wife), Maggie, who is also a great dancer, would jive with him. The result was a joy to behold as his nimble feet and safe hands swung the ecstatic young lady round and round, treating the chaps to a glimpse of her well-shaped, stocking-clad legs, while he, with a look of determined concentration, grinned broadly.

Maggie and Laurie were indeed very good pals. His, "Fancy a sherbet? Can you stand a large one?" was his way of inviting her to participate in a little beverage. She was his guinea pig for new jokes and material he had written, always being rewarded by his "You're a Good House, Mags!" whenever she responded in the way he had hoped.

In later years, he married April and fathered a child, Cindy, who became a little sister to his step-daughter Sherrie (April's child by a previous marriage). As little girls they were delightful. April was Freddie Randall's daughter. I was glad to see them settle down in Edgware, after her troubled earlier years. Their hospitality was legendary. Invited for Sunday lunch or for dinner at other times when you were available, you would be expected to stay the night. Laurie had a wonderful collection of records and books, reference and otherwise, and his knowledge of jazz and films was remarkable. He was also a very good conversationalist on almost any subject, and could hold you spellbound and, at the same time, listen to and accept your opinion with great interest. His seemingly endless hospitality for me always included a Churchill Havana double-corona cigar to accompany his generous measures of whisky or gin.

In the late 1970s, Laurie moved home. For the first time in his life he seemed to make an error of judgement, buying a bit of a pig-in-a-poke. I never saw the house, but I believe it cost him a fortune to make habitable to his standards. It was renamed 'Grey Friars', after the fictional school of another of his heroes, the gregarious Billy Bunter.

Laurie was never the same after Alex's death. He seemed to lose half of his being. He gave up drinking, cut down on his smoking and went to ground. Apart from a couple of visits to his shop, and one or two spasmodic phone calls, we hardly saw anything of each other. When I heard of his fatal accident, I at first refused to believe it, thinking there must be another explanation, such as his having engineered the whole affair. I don't believe this to be the case. Laurie was too extrovert and, although there were problems in his marriage, he loved his family too much to do anything stupid. When his will was read out, I was thrilled and proud to find out he had left me his guitar, the almost complete works of novelist Gerald Kersh (whose writings, as I have previously intimated, we both enjoyed immensely), and his collection of opera records, all in pristine condition. Although it was some time before I actually received my inheritance, due to a contesting of the will, I am now in possession of my personal memories of a dear friend with whom I am proud to have walked this Earth.

CHAPTER NINETEEN

THE END OF THE BEGINNING AND THE
BEGINNING OF THE END

Great things sometimes have an unhappy ending and the Alex Welsh Band proved to be no exception. For a while we enjoyed false tabs, with the inclusion of the magnificent pianist, Brian Lemon, the only jazz bass guitarist in the business, Pete Skivington, and vibraphonist and drummer, Roger Nobes.

I first heard the wonderful Brian Lemon in the Establishment Club, home of 'Beyond the Fringe' stars, Peter Cook and Dudley Moore. Although it was really Dudley's trio that was supposed to provide the jazz in the bar, he was very often otherwise occupied and asked Brian to deputise. Months later, I moved into a room in a house occupied by several musicians including Brian, and our friendship was formed. He helped and encouraged me immensely in my musical education, never refusing a request to write down a chord sequence or exercise for me.

The Nottingham-born pianist had long been deeply into all forms of jazz and had become adept in all of them, so it was no surprise to me that, on Fred's departure, Brian accepted Alex's invitation to join the band. He was in his late thirties when he joined but, probably due to a thinning hairline and adventurous lifestyle, looked a little older. He was a heavy smoker and drinker and, in fact, did everything to excess including, I am pleased to report, practising piano. Although late to bed most nights because of his gigs, he rose diligently at ten o'clock and, after a bout of heavy coughing from the first fag of the day and a cup of hot tea had encouraged some mandatory bodily functions, he would start his scales and exercises, breaking only to listen to and, sometimes, accompany, his heroes on recordings. Across the corridor, another fine pianist, Keith Ingham, was attending to similar chores. I found both of them inspiring. After a liquid lunch in the pub across the road, the practising would continue during the afternoon until it was time to eat and prepare for the evening gig.

Even with all this going on, Brian still had time for the ladies and, at one time, had three of them living with him in his room. Gloria was 'well stacked' as they say, and glamorous with it, but I think earned her wages from the oldest profession. Slim and blonde, the second, whose name escapes me, had several personal problems and left to return to Wales. Debbie eventually married Brian and bore him a son, Ian, a very likeable chap.

Unfortunately, shortly after Brian joined the band the couple went their different ways. Brian kept his flat in Ealing and went on to inherit some of Fred's piano-loving female friends, as well as encouraging new relationships with others of the same ilk.

Brian enjoyed being with the chaps and joined in our cricketing adventures and attempts at golf, with relish. On one trip to Kendal, Brian and I had arranged to play a round the next morning, and to this purpose, we had set an alarm call for seven-thirty, with tea and toast before we set off. Of course, we had forgotten the hospitality of Rita, the German landlady of the hotel and we were still drinking at four o'clock in the morning. I eventually bade Brian (who was still clutching a well-filled brandy glass), 'Goodnight'. I arose with the alarm and fully expected to make my way to the links alone but, to my surprise, Brian was already in the breakfast room, glass still in hand. We drove to the club, teed off and eventually reached the first green after hitting several poor shots and ascending a steep hill. A coughing, spluttering pianist reached for his putter but, as he did so, much to my astonishment, he raised the same glass, still half full, its having travelled securely in his bag, wedged by his clubs. He murmured, "This is what I've been looking forward to all the way up that blasted hill. Cheers, dear boy!"

Brian had a close friend in Ian Nicholl, an automobile electronics wizard, who had made a great deal of money from an invention he had designed for the Formula One racing teams. He was a Yorkshire man, but had lost his accent somewhere along the way – probably at public school – without realising it. I often heard him query, "Can't you tell I'm a 'tyke' from the way I speak?" in beautifully rounded Oxford tones.

The third member of this triumvirate was the wonderful tenor sax player, Danny Moss, who was also a fine golfer. A match at Biggin Hill's Cherry Lodge Golf Club was arranged between the three of us. It was more of a little needle match between Danny and I, as we played off similar handicaps, but Brian wanted to join in, while Ian kept our seats warm in the 'nineteenth' hole. Half way round, the call of nature struck Danny and, with no amenities in sight, he suffered a slight accident. His concentration started to waver and, by the eighteenth hole, I had clawed back a two-hole deficit to be 'all square' on the tee.

Ian had joined us and, somehow or other, I found myself with a short putt to win the match, which I duly sank.

"He hed you thair, Denny!" Ian's 'Yorkshire' voice bellowed across the green, much to the annoyance of a seething saxophonist.

When Brian's fortieth birthday arrived, we were in Aberystwyth. On booking into the hotel we were amazed to be welcomed by a waiter bearing a bottle of Champagne and seven glasses.

"I never thought I'd make it," was the pianist's explanation, "Cheers Chaps!"

The next year, ditto! What a guy! I am happy to say that Brian is still fooling himself, being in his seventies now, although, sadly, due to rheumatoid arthritis, he is unable to play. After leaving the band we worked together in many combinations and on several recordings. I consider myself among the very fortunate, who had the privilege to be a friend to one of the greatest jazz pianists who ever lived, anywhere or at any time.

My great friend, Pete Skivington, was already well established in the rhythm section before Brian joined, bringing his own wonderful sound and sense of time to the band. His zany sense of humour, and enjoyment of a 'throat salad' (his words) or two after-hours, slotted into the chaps' lifestyle perfectly, as did his fondness of a good animated discussion, his keen eye for a well-rounded bottom on a bicycle, and his talent for photography. He enjoyed creating new words for use, usually in an onomatopoeic sense, two of his favourites being 'swilllssshhh' to describe the sound of a real ale pump in operation, and 'llullbbb', that of a well-endowed lady removing her brassiere. He had also led a pop group named 'Batterin' Skelfer' (his stage name), at some time or another.

Pete's father was a Dundonian Scot, his mother of Welsh/Irish stock. He is to this day immensely proud of his heritage. Brought up in the London Borough of Enfield, young Peter was educated at the local grammar school, which listed among its most famous old boys a certain William Pratt, who was to become famous in Hollywood as Boris Karloff.

I first came across Pete in 1961 one Sunday lunchtime, when I was visiting a girlfriend, Janet Hughes, in a pub (of course) by a canal in Enfield. Pete knew her brother Roy, and we got talking. We hit it off immediately. This guy was right up my *Strasse*, as the say in Germany. Over the next year or two, whenever we met at places like Wood Green Jazz Club, we carried on our friendship as before. He joined the Terry Lightfoot band, which numbered among its ranks, Mickey Cooke and 'Barney' Bates, who were both to join Alex at a later date. This got him on the scene, bringing his talents to the notice of the jazz fraternity, although he had been associated with pianist Stan Greig, and making him the obvious choice to join the AW band when the time came. He had also joined Lennie's band, before the drummer's untimely stroke. Boy, did we have some fun!

Right from the start I found my soul-mate in the band. Don't get me wrong, everyone got along great, but there were partnerships. Alex and Fred were buddies; the Lancashire 'Likely Lads' had common interests in railways and cricket, and Lennie and I had spent a lot of time together, travelling and at the races. Harvey, with his interest in cars and who wasn't a regular drinker kept himself to himself much of the time.

When Pete joined, we all wondered how long he would be with us, for no other reason than he played bass guitar. I personally don't like the sound of most, but Pete's approach was different. No soft thumbing or fingering of the strings, but instead a good slap with a plectrum was his modus operandi and his instrument was different, also, in the fact that it was a semi-acoustic Hofner and not a plank of wood, like most. The result was as near as *dammit* the sound of a string bass, and boy, did he swing on it, with a great sense of time! After trying several orthodox bassists, Alex realised his rhythm section was once more complete.

Of course, our friendship, which had been founded a decade or so before, was now to be tested on a day-to-day basis. I need not have doubted for a moment that it would go from strength to strength, as we rediscovered our common likes and dislikes. We had the same taste in music, both liked cooking, enjoyed the friendly rivalry of our football teams (he Spurs, me Man U), had an eye for the fair lady and liked a beer or three. But it wasn't just me he blended with, fitting musically into the band and enjoying the same camaraderie and sense of humour as the rest of the chaps.

So, once again, the good ship 'Alex Welsh Band' sailed on trouble-free waters.

By 1972, Lennie's health had deteriorated so much that he had to depend on the rest of the band to load and unload his drums and his lack of energy began to affect his hitherto wonderful sense of time. After a particularly hard night at the Dixieland Pier, Blackpool, where we had appeared on a regular basis throughout the closed season for the Oolya Oolya Club, it was obvious that Len was knackered. It took an age for him to dismantle his drums, and we had to carry them to the wagon, where Harvey did his usual immaculate packing. Taking his place in the seat in the middle of the bus, we set off homeward. Len, I remember, struggling for breath, opened the side window just in front of Roy, who had (as was his usual custom), fallen asleep almost immediately.

"Shut the window please, Len; it's freezing!" the trombonist asked quietly.

"Bollocks!" came the reply.

"Oh, just be a little bit human!" said Roy.

"Human bollocks!" was the last words before the window was slammed shut.

Once again, a difficult decision had to be made by Alex and, in my opinion, he did the right thing and let Lennie go. I believe it probably extended his life for a couple of years. As for me, I lost my right-hand man, inspiration and friend, and the good ship the 'Alex Welsh Band' lost its chief engineer. So, in my humble opinion, the end of the beginning and the beginning of the end was born.

Several fine drummers were approached and auditioned; all great players, but somehow not quite right for the band. Alex even tried to get Ron McKay, who had impressed him greatly while with Acker Bilk, but he turned down the offer, saying he didn't feel he was good enough to fill Len's shoes. That was a pity in my opinion.

A 'Sing-along-a-Dixie' gig was coming up, which demanded the right kind of two-beat drumming required for the idiom, but not the kind of venue that critics would crawl from under stones to slate the band. Vibraphonist, Roger Nobes, who has already figured in another chapter, offered his services and. although having never heard him drum (or as I pointed out, didn't even know he owned a kit), Alex decided to give him a go.

The gig was a success and the bandleader was duly impressed by the drummer's approach (although lacking technique) of laying down a good foundation for the dancers in the crowd to take to the floor in numbers. He, of course, had another couple of weapons up his sleeve in his ability to read and arrange music, and his astounding talent on the vibraphone. Alex offered him the drum chair.

Over the next few months, the sound and repertoire of the band changed, as bossa nova and popular songs such as 'Wave' and 'By the Time I Get to Phoenix' were adapted to incorporate vibraphone, trombone and flute, respectively and added to the band repertoire. Harvey brought along a bass guitar, and John and I took turns at the drums.

Roger fitted in well with the chaps, although he could be a little sullen and moody at times. Brian and he (and later myself) were, of course, members of Dave Shepherd's fine quintet and sextet and they brought some of that style to the band, which delighted me as a long time devotee to the genius of Charley Christian. He also transcribed a couple of Buddy Rich and Count Basie numbers for the band, which were featured on later recordings. In lighter moments, he worked out great harmony for the chaps to sing on numbers like 'Toot Toot Tootsie' and 'Tie a Yellow Ribbon', which audiences loved.

So the beginning had ended but, surely, here was a new beginning? With Brian and Skiv, we once more had a tight rhythm section and the front line went from strength to strength. So, 'why the beginning of the end?', I hear you ask.

Alex, by this time, was drinking too much and his health was deteriorating to the extent that he was becoming slightly lethargic in his efforts on and off the stand; he had taken to staying up drinking too late in hotels, and falling into a melancholy nostalgia for his early band. Although I have no proof and, even if I did have, would never reveal his identity, I believe Alex was encouraged along these lines by someone in the band, who also liked to stay up late.

For some inexplicable reason, the first curtain fell on John Barnes. Chinese whispers circulated to the disbelief of the chaps. It took some time for the deed to be done as Alex (according to his wife Maggie), hummed and hawed and weighed up the consequences. By this time, we believed John had notions that all was not well. Eventually, the dark day arrived. So, the first nail was hammered into the coffin lid. To me, one of the greatest baritone, alto saxophone and clarinet players in British jazz, superb entertainer and humourist and all-round great fellow, got his marching orders.

Al Gay was, of course, the logical replacement, having already been a member of the early line-up. He had disposed of his nursing homes and retired to a cottage life in Bedfordshire. Al, of course, was also able to perform beautiful solo features, especially ballads, on the tenor saxophone, but was also adept on clarinet, soprano sax and flute. His slightly melancholy facial expression belied a wicked sense of humour, which included the delivery of corny one-liners in a hangdog manner, but ending with his whole face lighting up in a broad grin when he saw he was hitting the spot.

Born into an East-end Jewish family, Al Buchbinder was married at a very early age to Rose, whose family had arranged marriage to the young man to expedite her safe escape from the oncoming Holocaust in Hitler's Germany. His name, at some stage, was changed to Gay, which somewhat belied the sadness of his usual expression, but fully endorsed the mirth in his eyes when he laughed. (He later remarked that it was just his luck that homosexuals had used his adopted surname, resulting in telephone calls asking if he was A Gay.)

The young couple settled down and a daughter, Sandra, was born to them. They had set up home in Gants Hill, near Ilford, and the young clarinettist soon came to the attention of notables such as Joe Daniels and Freddie Randall, with whom he travelled to America as a union exchange for Bill Haley and his Comets. In the trad boom, he joined Bob Wallis's 'Storeyville' Jazz Band, with their Southern Gentlemen's knee-length frock coats and Mississippi gamblers' hats. One member of Bob's band recalled Al's sense of humour when, at one gig, he had played a clarinet solo on his knees, resembling Toulouse L'Autrec and breaking his clarinet in the middle to resemble a snake emerging from a charmer's basket. On another occasion, when he'd had to wear a loudly coloured striped waistcoat for some Dixieland function, he had described his attire as 'just like a Jewish deck-chair!'

I worked with Al a couple of times before he re-joined the band. He was the proprietor of a small cafe in Gant's Hill, which he sold to buy a nursing home in Windsor, where he was able to use his skills as a qualified physiotherapist and still have enough spare time to indulge in his jazz gigs.

Off and on through my time with the band, Alex used Al to compliment the front line when the fee would cover the expense, and he was indeed a welcome addition. The already rich sound of the band became that of a roaring lion with him on form, as he invariably was. Thus, he had re-joined the band when John left, as I have already stated. During this period the band undertook a short tour of Denmark, starting and finishing in Copenhagen. We stayed, believe it or not, in the hotel Rosendahl (Rose and Al), which was a tall, round edifice consisting of several storeys with rooms on the outer wall serviced by circular corridors. At points on the wall of these corridors were payphones from which we could dial directly home. We had performed a Sunday lunchtime gig and were resting up in anticipation of the jazz club appearance in the evening. Before leaving home, Al and Rose had had 'words' and, during the tour, weren't exchanging many between them. They owned a beautiful German Shepherd, called Shane, who went everywhere with them and whom Al adored. This particular afternoon the silence, apart from the gentle snoring of the recumbent chaps, was broken by the sound of Krone being entered into a payphone, followed by Al's deep voice saying, "Hello! Yes, all right! Can I talk to Shane? "Hellloooo Boooyyy!" (bark, bark) "Have you been a good boy?"

I heard Roy in the next room begin to chortle. Later he explained that he couldn't get the picture out of his head of an angry woman holding the phone to the ear of the dog, while her non-communicative husband ignored her in favour of the animal!

For a few months, things seemed all right but, gradually, I sensed a little unrest in Roy Williams and, so, it was no surprise to me that, when Humphrey Lyttelton, who was now employing John, came knocking, Roy was off.

How do you replace Roy Williams? You can't, of course. But. on a positive side, there were several excellent trombonists queuing up to join the 'best band in the land'. Alex didn't rush into a replacement. Several well-documented players were tried over the next few gigs, such as Jim Shepherd, Campbell Burnap and George Howden, but the chair went to Mickey Cooke, who, as Roy had done, left Terry Lightfoot to join.

For the next few months or so, stability returned to the band, even a sense of refreshing excitement, due to the Dixieland approach that Alex desired, and the front line was able to deliver.

Mickey brought his own exciting style to the front line. He had passed the drinking test with A-levels, and had settled into his first seminar as an Alex Welsh band freshman like a fish takes to water or, in his case, cider, Guinness, beer, or whatever. Skiv and Mick had served their apprenticeships in pubs and such with the Lightfoot band, so the time had come for graduation into the guild of masterful imbibers, of which I had become a director. A triumvirate of raving hooligans was formed, as we laughed and boozed in the after-hours life of the jazzer. It wasn't to last. Rumours started spreading that we were all to be replaced (in my case by Judd Procter, can you imagine?) and they seemed to emanate from the same source, which I am sure you, dear reader, will be able to pinpoint for yourself.

One by one, the band broke up: Brian, then Skiv and Mickey, all went for different reasons. Ron Rubin and Brian Leake, followed by Colin Bates, came into the picture. Another story went about that Roy Crimmins wanted to re-join, which he duly did. Laurie Chescoe joined and Denny Wright and Dave Cliff got cameo roles.

It was no longer for me. I became disillusioned and, as I had just experienced an unhappy divorce, I was considering moving back to Scotland. In the end, I stuck with it until the band, directly through Alex's illness, could no longer support me and I found other employment.

The beginning of the end had arrived!

CHAPTER TWENTY

THE COAL MERCHANT'S LADDIE

Alexander Welsh was born on the ninth of July, 1929, in the Port of Leith, an important suburb of the capital city of Edinburgh, on the south side of the Firth of Forth. The docks were busy with the exportation of whisky from the nearby bonded warehouses, agricultural products from the thriving countryside around the city and the importation of necessary products like fossil fuels, such as coal, from places such as Newcastle-upon-Tyne.

As far as I can find out, Alex's father ran a domestic coal delivery business, which was sufficiently successful to enable his family to enjoy a reasonably comfortable lifestyle in their flat in Lorne Square, just off Leith Walk, the main road from the city centre to the busy port.

Alex senior, a catholic by religion, had married a protestant, Ann Plank and the union had produced two children: Alex junior and his younger sister, Ann, (as you will realise, named after their parents and both brought up in the teachings of the Presbyterian Church of Scotland, at the insistence of their religiously-disillusioned father). Scotland, and Edinburgh in particular, which had seen the rise of Calvinism and John Knox, holds an unreasonable and perhaps unhealthy intolerance of Catholicism even to this day and, to protect his children from any unnecessary bigotry, he had decided on this action, even to the extent of turning visiting priests from his door.

Alex seems to have enjoyed a normal, healthy childhood, with the usual interests and hobbies indulged in by a child of the thirties: reading, stamp collecting and sport and, especially, football. The young Alex was, in fact, football crazy and what's more, he was good at it. So good, in fact, that he had been approached by Raith Rovers and, I believe, signed schoolboys' forms of contract with the famous club. Imagine, then, the unbelievable disappointment he must have experienced when, at the age of nine or ten, he suffered the accident that shattered his dreams and football ambitions for good. He took a tackle, which badly grazed his right knee, but wasn't considered sufficiently bad to stop the family from hurrying to the cinema in their haste to catch the beginning of a film.

Perhaps the wound merited more attention than it received, but boys are boys and the pictures, especially if they featured his boyhood hero, Al Jolson, whose films he had devoured time and again, were far more important than a scratch on the knee. Whatever the cause, an infection got into the wound and this developed into osteomyelitis, a debilitating bone disease that inhibited the natural growth of his right leg. Nowadays, an antibiotic would have taken care of such bacteria, but this accident happened in the days before penicillin and other such wonder drugs. I know his poor mother blamed herself for not dressing the wound properly but after all, how many knocks and bumps does a young chap take in the process of growing up? I think she was much too hard on herself.

So young Alex was hospitalised in a spinal couch, in plaster from the chest down for eighteen months and his football playing days came to an end. During further convalescence at home and in his teenage years, he turned his attention to education, for which he achieved a Higher Leaving Certificate with distinction and to his love for music. I have mentioned his fondness of Al Jolson, but have to tell you that his whole family, especially his father (who played the accordion and was known as the 'Pied Piper of Leith'), were music mad. Hours were spent listening to Radio Luxembourg, with its featured crooners and their popular songs, with the young man and his dad harmonising in the background.

He joined the Boys' Brigade, where he learned to blow the bugle, progressing to a silver cornet as his musical prowess developed. In 1945, he found employment in the legal department of the Scottish Widows Life Assurance Society, became a keen golfer, and practised his cornet diligently. On his twenty-first birthday he couldn't decide between a new set of clubs or a trumpet.

At this stage, I must mention how indebted I am to Alex's Edinburgh sweetheart, Frances, who, in later years was associated with the Edinburgh Jazz Festival, and who has furnished me with a lot of the information you have just read. I think it would be fitting and, indeed, delightful to let her describe the next stage in her own words:

"It didn't take long, therefore, before Alex started to seek out others who might be bitten by the jazz bug and when clarinettist, Archie Semple, advertised for a trombone player, Alex went along with a friend who auditioned (unsuccessfully) for the chair. Alex had brought along his silver cornet, which, until then, he had only publicly played in the Boys Brigade Band, and there and then secured himself a place in Archie's band, replacing the band leader's brother, who preferred playing piano anyway, the trombone chair being filled by Dave Keir. Thus the Archie Semple Capitol Jazz Band was formed and quickly became the foremost Chicago-style band in Scotland.

"Alex was therefore devastated when, in 1952, Archie left for London to join Mick Mulligan's Magnolia Jazz Band. However, with his usual determination, Alex, with Davy Keir and clarinettist, Jackie Graham, set about forming the Nova Scotia Jazz Band.

"The next to go 'down south' in 1953 was Al Fairweather and Alex was asked to replace him in the Sandy Brown Band, which despite the change in style, he did with great success.

"In the early to mid-1950s, Alex spent most of his spare time practising and listening to the great horn players, never dreaming that some of them would soon be guests in his band! He also paid great attention to the stagecraft of visiting musicians; all this in preparation for the huge step of moving to London on the 4th of May, 1954."

I have heard a few different versions as to what happened on Alex's arrival in the capital. I do know for certain that he did some work with Mick Mulligan, as second trumpet, and it was at this time that George Melly christened him 'The Lemonade King', as a reference to – unusual for a jazz musician – his abstinence from alcohol. There were also rumblings of unrest in the Freddie Randall band, which, at the time, boasted among its ranks Archie, Roy Crimmins and Len Hastings. Alex was approached to see whether he would be interested in joining a breakaway outfit. Having agreed that he was, it was decided to draw lots as to who would lead the new band. Alex, as he always maintained, 'drew the short straw', to the disappointment, I believe, of Roy, who had fancied the position. This band should not be confused with the great band that performed at the Royal Festival Hall concerts organised by Harold Pendleton; classics in their own right.

This, indeed, was the band (with the exception of John Richardson on drums, later replacing Lennie Hastings, who had joined Johnnie Duncan's Blue Grass Boys, and Bill Reid on bass), that I heard for the first time as a callow youth in Edinburgh's Princes Street Gardens. It was the same outfit with Lennie back, and Tony Pitt replacing Diz Disley, or Neville Skrimshire, that I met in London in the 'Trad boom', when I joined the Clydes. It was recognisably musically different from the majority of the bands of the 'trad fad' era, and its members were, for the most part, held in great respect by their contemporaries.

My own personal impression of Alex was a little unfavourable at first. Oh yes, he could play all right, but did he have to wear that incessant false-looking smile and did he ever mix with anyone, including his own band members? I remember approaching him at an all-nighter in Birmingham Town Hall, hoping for a little chat as a fellow Scot and Edinburgh musician but, in answer to my sincere words of appreciation of his band he replied, "Thanks Laddie!" and turned away.

Although ambitious, I had no confidence of ever joining his band at that time and was, indeed, quite in awe of Tony and, of course, the great Diz Disley. When my chance came I grasped it with both hands and this has been adequately chronicled in the opening chapter.

Alex did have buddies, though, in people like Laurie Ridley, Phil Robertson, Jim Godbolt, the wonderful Ruby Braff, and of course, Wild Bill Davison. He was well respected as a fine lead trumpet player and bandleader among fellow musicians, agents and promoters alike, but most of his intimate friends were women. He was quite a ladies' man and (before meeting and eventually marrying Maggie), had 'friends' all over the country. For the most part I believe he treated them admirably, but I don't think he could have been easy to live with. Anyway, that is nobody's business but his.

One can only take as one finds and, for the best part of eighteen years, I did just that. I am left with hundreds of wonderful memories, musical and otherwise, some of which I have already conveyed in other chapters of this book and some I will attempt to rescue from the furthest reaches of the part of my brain that stores such things, in an attempt to convey them to you now. There are those that flood the memory as soon as any reference to the band comes into a conversation, while others need jogging, or hit you when least expected, like in the middle of the night when you get home from a poor gig and the memory of a great one helps to dissipate your frustration and enable sleep.

The Newport concert is one of the former. Hardly a day passes when some thing or someone doesn't trigger the memory of that wonderful evening, and, indeed, bring the whole experience flooding back. Inevitably, the evening that the Basie Band was performing has to be another and, being a little late on arrival, we all started running towards the auditorium from whence the wonderful sound was emanating, Alex included. The Dresden Concert is a third; what some people consider to be the best recording the band ever made was almost destroyed by an on-stage argument between Alex and Roy, about (believe it or not), the acoustic of the hall. Then there were the impromptu, after-gig piss-ups in hotels, when the band performed their party pieces, like John and Roy singing 'Barefoot Days', Harvey wailing through Victorian tear-jerkers in a broad Cockney accent and, above all, Alex and Lennie harmonising, 'You are my Heart's Delight', while standing on chairs, trousers rolled up to the knee and half-crown monocles screwed into their eyes.

Indeed, it only took a mere suggestion to get Alex leading a barbershop quartet. John, Roy, Skiv and the leader were the main harmonisers, with the rest of us putting our penny's worth in from a distance. Sometimes Jack Peacock (who is the brother of Dave, of Chas and Dave fame and a great friend of the band), would take part and was good for laying down a strong melody, a role often fulfilled by Maggie in later years.

When I first joined the band I felt a little patronised by the leader, considering the difference in our age and experience, but this soon turned to welcoming kindness towards me and Ron Mathewson , who had felt the same as me. When he realised that we could offer something to the band – and even understand the type of jazz he adored so much – we were treated with much greater respect, even to the extent of raising our basic wage to a par with the rest of the guys, as long as we kept it quiet from Herr Len, who always believed one should be paid according to experience.

Ron and I found a nice flat in West Kensington, one stop on the tube from Earl's Court, where Alex lived. The first Sunday after we had taken up residence, we were invited to Sunday lunch, where we were treated to succulent roast beef and a hitherto, on my part, untried delicacy of Yorkshire pudding, cooked to perfection by Carol, his lovely partner.

Perhaps the time is right to explain Alex's marital status (although, as I have already stated, really is nobody's business), which I, personally, feel had a lot to do with his attitude to women in general and, in my humble opinion, a slight feeling of personal insecurity he tried to disguise with his natural good looks and position as a band leader.

On leaving Edinburgh, Alex had also left behind his fiancée, Frances, whom you have already met in this chapter. I believe the separation to have been a sudden decision on the part of the former and a tremendous shock to the latter. In London, he seemed to find it easy to put his past behind him, finding the availability of partners plentiful and he soon found himself wooing and marrying a lady called Nicky. I can't say what went wrong, but I do know from various reliable sources that both partners played away from home and the marriage failed. From either petulance or perhaps downright cussedness, or a combination of both on his part, Alex refused to divorce his estranged partner. You must remember that, at that time, a divorce was legally much more difficult to obtain, and I believe he wanted the world to think that he was the wronged party inasmuch as it was alright for a man to have other lovers, but not a woman.

He became a 'Dapper Dan', a ladies' man, and Carol was one of his 'conquests'. This partnership lasted for a couple of years, during which I think he grew more and more restless and, eventually, it ended in an acrimonious separation. Carol was a sweet, attractive Irish girl with dark hair and bright blue eyes, not really Alex's ideal feminine formula of skinny, gamine, and blonde, and I felt he once again was a bit cruel in his decision to part from her, causing her to suffer a nervous breakdown.

So that takes care of that.

It soon became clear that Alex's idea of a successful band involved teamwork. His love of football was undiminished. He was a fervid supporter of Celtic and his pride knew no boundaries when, to a man, the band watched his heroes become the first British winners of the European Cup in the lounge of the Fox and Hounds pub in Haywards Heath, Sussex. He compared the band to a good winning team, with himself as the captain. He expected the players to perform with both heart and, as he put it, 'bollocks', a major factor in his considerations when hiring or firing his musicians. Often, at the conclusion of a successful gig or tour, he would say, "Well done, team!" He was, of course, a good captain: in my opinion, the best lead trumpet player this country has ever produced, and one of the fairest bandleaders.

His democracy extended to letting the chaps play solos and features in their chosen style and he encouraged humour as part of the band make-up. Financially he was among the fairest men I ever knew, taking only a small extra wage for running the band and holding enough cash in a fund to pay bonuses at the times of the year when they were most appreciated. He delegated chores to those in the band willing to accept them, such as keeping a subs book, driving, booking hotels, and the like.

He wore a difficult shell to crack but, when he did take it off, he was humorous, generous and one of the lads. Some of the time he was sullen, distant and a pain in the arse and could display a cynicism that was quite hurtful. I know he suffered a good deal of discomfort and pain from his leg, especially when the band went on tour and, as his health declined, he showed a reluctance to leave the comfort of his home for any length of time. When we did, he relied on our road managers more and more. To the more ambitious in the band this became an understandable set back and disappointment in light of the reputation, quality, and worldwide demand for the band. Tours to Australia and India were promised, but never materialised and, on the first day of short domestic or European tours, Alex would annoy the chaps by offering, "Never mind, chaps, we'll be home in a few days!" before we had even had half a chance to get into the tour. Living out of a suitcase is part and parcel of touring, just as renewing old acquaintances and discovering new cities is and some of us looked forward to the adventure of it all.

Influences inside and outside of the band eventually led to his letting John Barnes go, quickly followed by Roy Williams, to be replaced by Al Gay and, eventually, Roy Crimmins, in a (in my opinion misguided) move to resurrect the Dixieland approach of his earlier band. Couldn't John and Roy play Dixieland? There is plenty of recorded proof of their ability to do so. By the late seventies, gigs were becoming sparser and Alex's health was seriously deteriorating. I had to find other sources of income and did so by working with Dave Shepherd, Pete Allen and Keith Smith and indulging in my other love of cooking. None of it even remotely measured up to the best days I spent with Alex Welsh and nothing to this day has.

Alex

CHAPTER TWENTY ONE

TOURS AND TRAVELITIS

An essential part of a band's ability to exist was to undertake tours at home and indeed abroad. As motorways and A-roads improved, the boundaries for driving home from one night stands became farther from the capital but, in the early days I am covering in this chronicle, two or three-week tours of the country were commonplace. I have described the problems this caused in the logistic sense in my chapter on transport, but other problems, domestic, financial, and matrimonial, presented themselves from time to time.

Hours of tedium were omnipresent. Dining in not-too-salubrious transport cafes was an essential time saving necessity, booking into and staying in age-weary terraced-house hotel conversions economically mandatory and an overriding ability to enjoy ones travelling companions was a great bonus.

Further down the page I will describe how lucky we were in the latter category and how we coped with the former, but they were always hard to swallow, if you will excuse the pun.

A typical tour would consist of various types of gigs, usually centred round one or two well-paid concerts or company balls, interspersed with less financially, but more musically, rewarding jazz clubs, to make the journeys and fuel costs manageable. The rewards were obvious, the well-paid jobs paying the mortgage and the clubs giving you the chance to let your hair down musically, to renew old acquaintances and form new friendships with local musicians and jazz lovers. Among the band's favourite venues, I can pick half a dozen where we were always more than heartily welcomed: Birmingham and the Second City Jazz Band, Manchester and the MSG, Kendal and the Les Bull Band, Nottingham's 'Dancing Slipper', Liverpool and the Merseysippee Band, Leeds and the Yorkshire Cricketers, Wolverhampton and Tommy Burton, and Derby's Corporation Hotel; and abroad: Berlin, Dusseldorf, Stuttgart, Zurich and Paris and festivals in Nice, Copenhagen and Prague, as well as fine clubs in Brussels, Scheviningen, near The Hague and, of course, Newport, Rhode Island - all exciting new cities and venues offering friendship and experiences I, for one, will never forget. We also went on tour behind the Iron Curtain several times, but that experience deserved its own chapter and has duly been given one.

Everywhere we travelled, we made new friendships and I am glad to say some of them have endured the cruel passage of the years and are still renewed from time to time.

For those friendships that are no longer possible to be continued, I am sure I can speak for the band in thanking them for their contributions to our lives. It wouldn't have been the same without them.

Nowadays, much can be done to while away the hours travelling, with the availability of personal CD players, televisions, audio and electronic books and laptop computers. In the heyday of the band, reading books, filling in crossword puzzles, and playing card games or Scrabble were the only options open to the itinerant musician. We also indulged in a couple of competitive team games, including one called 'Legs'. This consisted of splitting the travellers into two sides, left and right, and amassing points by collecting 'legs' from pub signs (Red Lion, two legs; Horse and Jockey, six; Coach and Horses, eight, etc.) Beware 'Arms', however – an automatic loss of two legs; 'Head' lost four, and worst of all 'Rose and Crown', where you lost all your legs and had to start again. Before motorways, this was a great way to pass miles on single-carriageway roads.

The second game was much more unsubtle and probably to some readers slightly disgusting, but it has to be noted here for the sheer fun and discomfort it offered to the chaps. It was based on farting. Indelicate as it may seem to you, there is no other way to describe it. This time the coach was split into two teams; those occupying the middle row of seats and those in the rear. Alex in the front seat with the driver didn't get involved. There was no time scale for 'Fart Football', inasmuch as you could score at any time. Scoring involved a member of a team surreptitiously passing wind noiselessly, and without telling the members of the opposition. If the odour from the fart reached over the seat in either direction and was met by a howl of anguish, a goal was scored. The resulting action was usually the lighting of cigarettes or pipes by those scored against.

The team in the back won its own World Cup one day. While the band was travelling homeward from Germany and was passing through Canterbury in the midst of a thunderstorm and torrential downpour John Barnes suddenly 'let one go'. Immediate retching and gasping for breath broke out among the ranks; he nearly scored an own goal! The smell even reached the driver, Jeff Garrard.

"Stop the wagon!" someone shouted from the front. Jeff pulled in to the side of the road, double yellow lines and all, and the chaps fell out of the bus gasping for air – even Alex – while Boko chortled in his seat. Five minutes later, seven soggy and one dry passenger set off once more.

On other occasions, attempts at discussion would often end in arguments among the travellers. Downright obstinacy caused by too much booze, or the cantankerousness that emanates from weariness, was often the cause. No different from any organisation, we naturally had fall-outs among ourselves, but I am pleased to report that, for the most part, the guys got on pretty amicably. The common denominator was, of course, humour.

We shared the same sense of eccentric lunacy emanating from such role models as wartime favourite Tommy Hanley and his successful ITMA show, the Goon Show, Laurel and Hardy and the Marx Brothers. Added to this was the artist's ability for keen observation of his fellow man, and his sometimes less-than-gentle mimicry of the same, together with a certain degree of boyishness that seems to be inherent in the male character whenever several are ganged together. Forced to spend long periods of time in our own company, the immaturity of the Welsh Band manifested itself in the form of boyish slapstick and nonsense, which came to be known as 'Travel-itis'.

The main perpetrators were John and Roy, egged on and ably aided and abetted by Fred, who delighted in getting an easily tempted Lennie to swallow the bait. The drummer was the owner of an incredible, hearty, infectious laugh, and he would collapse into helpless, almost tearful fits which, time after time, brought the whole show literally to a stop. At some stage in his extraordinary life, he had enjoyed a little masochistic pleasure from visits to a sadistic lady known professionally as Anita Wyplash. Roy played on this knowledge by inventing a fictional, middle class Hooray Henrietta, who was supposedly enamoured with Len. At a quiet moment on a journey he would lean across to the drummer, seated immediately in front of him and in a low, George Sanderson-like voice, say something like, "What was her name? Ah, yes, Lady Cynthia Thrashbuttocks, of Number 24 the Lashes, Much-Whippington-on-Ouse, Herts. Yes! That's it! I'm sure you would take great pains to see her again! Stop punishing yourself and call her, you naughty boy!"

Unable to contain himself, Herr Len would collapse holding his sides and pleading for Roy to, "Stop it, for Gawd's sake, stop it!"

At this point Fred would throw coals on the fire by adding, "Come on Len! You know she really fancies you and can't wait to get her hands on you!"

All the while the rest of the chaps imitated the sound of whip lashes and uttered horrendous cries of pain and anguish, resulting in Herr Hastings ending up writhing on the wagon floor in helpless belly-aching, side-clutching, ecstatic agony.

Len had brought his own style of humour to the public eye by way of his 'cod' versions of German drinking songs, Lehar classics and his send-ups of Adolf Hitler and Richard Tauber, but little is known of his private obsession with them and, indeed, Winston Churchill. I have described my Christmas morning experience at his home, but failed in my duty to inform you that the triumvirate accompanied him everywhere on our travels through the medium of reel-to-reel tapes. Space in the wagon had to be found for two Grundig reel-to-reel tape recorders and a small Globe Trotter suitcase, as well as the necessary travel pack. As soon as the suitcase was deposited in his hotel room it exploded, showering the room with WW2 paraphernalia. Swastika armbands, Iron Crosses, stage make-up and discarded toupees, dyed black, festooned the furniture like Christmas decorations and dead rodents. Heaven knows what he got up to when alone.

By the early 1970s, another obsession had entered his life, inspired by the Beatles, Stones and the parodies by the Barron Knights, Bonzo Dog Doodah Band, etc. He *knew* he could write a hit song! If he was not able to compose the music he could at least come up with some funny words to an existing melody. In 1971, the Minister of Transport, Barbara Castle, introduced the breathalyser test for drinking and driving which, for a while, made her the most unpopular lady in the land. What this meant to the hard-drinking travelling jazz musicians, you can well imagine, but it offered our budding chart-topper a fool-proof theme for his parody. Borrowing Dvorak's 'Humoresque', he came up with what he reckoned would be a guaranteed number one.

We were recording for Polydor at that time and Alex had decided to issue a single of 'If I had a Talking Picture of You'.

Reluctantly, after a great deal of persuasion from the originator of the 'Twickenham Sound', Alex agreed to put the Breathalyser Song on the 'B' side. It was actually quite amusing, sung as it was, with a Cockney accent (at one point the subject of the song tries to disguise his breath by eating 'one rawrunyan') and ending with a nod in the direction of the Beatles' Scouse, with the words, "I'll swing fer 'im, ya know dat!" Unfortunately, neither the 'A' nor the 'B' side got anywhere close to number one.

But the real king of travel madness had to be John Barnes. Anyone who remembers the band will have seen and heard his comic genius in his monologues and hilarious vocals, but few will have any idea just how eccentric he could be in real life. From early photographs of him pulling faces to emulate his boxer dog, Dobbin (in which he succeeded brilliantly), to his love of Music Hall and Vaudeville, and grown-up toys, John produced a gold mine of merry quips and wheezes.

It was he who introduced crazy foam custard pies to the stage at Wood Green Jazz Club, prior to the fun foam-filled aerosols grabbing the imagination of the country. What started by a paper plate of foam being thrust into his own face finished up in complete madness, as each of the chaps in turn received the same treatment and returned it with glee. Just as in the old black and white slapstick movies, musicians, instruments, and the stage itself ended up covered in the stuff. It even landed on selected members of the audience.

It was he who, as a lover of acronyms and spoonerisms, created new names for the chaps, such as Dum Jig-less! Not content with even this, I eventually became 'Can't speak, can't dance'. Think about it...

It was John who, at the time we were involved in charity cricket matches with members of the Yorkshire cricket team against a side made up of West Ham and Tottenham Hotspur footballers, captained by the great Jimmy Greaves, travelled for mile after mile wearing a cricketer's box on the outside of his trousers, while, at the same time, sporting batting gloves holding a cricket ball, 'just to get used to them'. (As an aside, some years later, Maggie and I were discussing cricket and this box story came up:

"Did you know I often wondered what that was?" Maggie said, (her having previously seen a pink plastic thing in a brown paper bag at a cricket match, where she was keeping score). "I thought it was a jelly mould!"

It couldn't have been any other than John, having discovered and taken to practising yoga, who shocked and startled a hotel chambermaid, when, on entering his room to turn down his bed, she discovered him standing on his head, naked as the day he was born!

It was John, of course, who acquired the aforementioned 'Guidaye', and altered an old passport for 'him' to enable 'his' travel to East Germany, where 'he' had a wonderful time changing the personalities of fans all over that Country.

Of all John's toys, the one I will remember forever was, in fact, not so much a toy as a quite sophisticated, battery-operated radio-cassette recorder, which he produced at the start of one tour. Over the next couple of weeks he recorded all sorts of nonsensical repartee and sketches, I hope for posterity.

Among the more memorable were Len's 'Luniar Module' (he was indeed slightly dyslexic, another of his favoured words being 'mechanichism'), inspired by the successful Apollo missions. The sketch starts with a countdown of ten, after which is heard the sound of a car struggling to start because of a faulty battery. The sound fades to a weary groan before a mighty explosion tears the air apart. Picture the scene: An American mission controller counts down to 'blast off'.

"Ten, nine, eight, seven...three, two, one...We have lift off!"

Rrrrr, rrr, rrrrrr...rrrr, rrrrr...rrr–rr-r...r, rr...rr -------r------- ---------r, r......

The battery goes flat! After a moment's silence one hears the sound of fierce blowing into the microphone to simulate an explosion and, "We have blast off!" followed by hoots of laughter as the rest of the chaps fall about.

Also on the tape you could hear Fred's gasp of horror as he portrays someone bidding farewell to friends as he walks backwards into a lift, which hasn't quite reached floor level. His yell of terror was so convincingly accurate, I still double-check lifts to this day.

Roy's contributions included a description of a musically dodgy organist he had heard demonstrating in a department store in Luton. To emulate the sound, he destroyed Hoagy Carmichael's beautiful 'Stardust', played on an out-of-tune piano we came across somewhere. John just had to get that down, thank goodness. Harvey completed the scene by announcing the piece, in an over-the-top American accent, as being performed by Antonio Roncordi! But it didn't end there: borrowing the recorder, Roy visited the store the very next weekend and, while his two boys diverted the organist's attention by feigning interest, he pointed the microphone, concealed in his overcoat, at the musician and recorded him for posterity. The resulting recording, of Herb Alpert's 'What's New', had a hilarious reception on being re-played to the band.

The band occasionally appeared at The Sherpa, a public house in Scunthorpe. On the way there we had to drive past a site where a product called 'dry slag' was produced by a manufacturer called Clugsten. Inevitably, Barnsie recorded us all trying to pronounce, "Get yer dra slag frum Clugsten's at Scoontherp!" in a Yorkshire accent. To add insult to injury, the hotel we stayed in was named the Cocked Hat, or as John insisted 'T'cock't'at'. It's all recorded on the tape; I do hope it still exists.

This might be a fitting moment to describe probably the worst meal I was ever offered, including the Spam curry the band was once treated to. As often was the case, we had stopped at a fish and chip shop to line our stomachs with blotting paper, before the evening's probable debauchery. We found one on the outskirts of Scunthorpe one evening, and filed in. There appeared to be only one portion of fish cooked and, rather than wait for fresh supplies, I agreed to buy it. I drew the short straw. Taking the newspaper wrapped package back to the bus, I took my seat and opened one end of it. Munching on a few chips I thought, *not bad at all*. Picking up the battered fish, I thought how hard and greasy it felt. I shook it and it rattled. Unwisely I sank my teeth into what resembled a leather wallet. Immediately spitting out my mouthful of foul-tasting cardboard, I inverted the packet. A shrivelled, dried-up, rock solid cube of what once had been cod, fell out. Heaven knows how often it had been re-cooked. I discarded the lot and settled for a sandwich and a pint at the pub.

The success of John's recordings grabbed the band's imagination. Suggestions and ideas were offered; some ludicrous and infantile, others really worthwhile and entertaining. I remember being interviewed on a windy corner in Whitley Bay on my hero, footballer Denis Law, and being shocked by the broadness of my Scottish accent. He committed us to tape trying to sound like a Lancashire Landlady we knew, by asking "D'ye wanta frrriieedd brekfist?" Roy related a story about a dreadfully hung over musician, who had woken up next to a none-too beautiful lady who enquired, "Did you mean it last night when you told me you loved me?" A grunt emanated from the other side of the bed. She then informed him that there was only one thing she wanted in life.

"What's that?" the suffering chap enquired, trying to cope with his 'iron turban'.

"To be your wife!" was her reply, to be followed by the sound of a closing door and footsteps running down the corridor accompanied by cries of anguish from the horrified musician.

So it continued.

Len played 'Out of Nowhere' on the piano in the style of Errol Garner. He informed us: "Ich bin der bestes Strassenbahn Fuehrer in ganzes grosses weld!"

I am the best tram driver in the whole world!

And, "Eins fur Ich, und eins fur Dich und eins fur Onkel Heinerich!"

It didn't stop at German either, when he offered a classic, which became known as Lennie's Language Lessons, inspired by the Linguaphone series.

These took the form of exercises in 'Spanish'.

Pronounced slowly at first in English, the sentence was followed by the translation in 'Spanish', and a gap for the learner to repeat the lesson. The subject of the lesson was a poor fellow down on his luck, but getting a lucky break, and went something like this.

Lesson one:

"The poor old tramp had neither money nor a job and was feeling very depressed."

"El trampo pooro haba nixo gelto, nixo jobbo, futura dismo. El choko! El choko!"

Lesson two:

"He had been searching the gutters all day for money but had found nothing."

"El looko guttero nighto dayo, gelto nixo findo. El skinto! El skinto!"

Lesson three:

"Suddenly he espied a wallet full of fifty pound notes lying on the pavement and jumped with joy."

"Subito looka downo espyo mucho loota! Newsuito, cigaro, largea gintonico, mucho grino. El sprontzo! El sprontzo!

It won't do anything for your Spanish, but it might give you a chuckle.

So that was travel-itis. Perhaps after all these years my memory is playing tricks and has led me to think it was funnier than it really was.

No, darn it, it was funny, bloody funny, and I wouldn't have missed it for the world.

It would be great to hear that tape again; just to hear the voices of those who are gone, if nothing more, would be wonderful.

If this chapter has read like a laundry list, I do beg your pardon, but it really was how things were; one item of nonsensical tomfoolery followed by another. But it was so wonderfully therapeutic and I am sure it kept us from going insane through the boredom of travelling.

Travel-itis wasn't confined to the bandwagon alone, however - it went everywhere with us, and I'm sure in some instances people must have considered us to be at the very least extremely childish, or more likely slightly bonkers. But it can save lives. Get a gang of your buddies together sometime and give it try; you will be amazed!

CHAPTER TWENTY TWO

WHEN THE END COMES...I KNOW...

I couldn't be around for some of Alex's last gigs. In a way, I am glad not to have been. Over the last two years of his life I had witnessed a steady deterioration in his health, manifesting itself in a yellowing of his skin and a premature ageing in his appearance. His playing was also suffering, as was to be expected in someone so desperately ill.

In 1980, I was devoting most of my time to playing with Keith Smith's Hefty Jazz, plus the odd gig here and there with other bands and pick-up groups. I was also working five mornings a week in a sandwich bar in Shepherd Market, with trombonist George Howden.

I know I missed a couple of Pizza Express sessions, but believe my place was ably filled by Dave Cliff,, and a broadcast, for which Alex had used the wonderful Denny Wright.

I do, however, know that I was with him on his last appearance at the 100 Club. He was painfully thin and had a worrying frailty, which gave me great concern for his well-being. It's ironic and fitting that my last gig with him should be in the theatre of his many triumphs; musical, social, and indeed sexual.

Before Alex met his second wife Maggie he was, as I have previously mentioned, known to be quite a ladies' man, and would entertain conquests, as he liked to think of them, all over the country. Always smartly dressed and groomed, with a permanent smile on his face when on the bandstand, he flirted continually. I suppose being the leader and available helped him in his success, but I also think he appeared extremely attractive to the opposite sex.

The 100 Club always provided a great evening for the band. Dozens of regular fans and friends always turned up and inspired the sessions. Laurie, Jack Peacock, John Morrow, Diz if he was free, Frank Parr, Ma and Pa Ling, Posh Pat, Brown-ale Pete, Jonah; the list goes on and on. It is, of course, of no importance to you, dear reader, but was an integral, immensely essential, part of our success at the 'Hundred'. It was the Mecca for musicians, whether being free on the evening, or on the way to or returning from a gig, and therefore a superb place for the chaps to exchange gigs, anecdotes, and news.

It was therefore not unexpected when the phone rang and a broken-hearted Laurie Ridley told me that Alex had been admitted to Hillingdon Hospital. Maggie, herself, was having alcohol problems and had been voluntarily admitted to a detoxification and rehabilitation centre, about ten days previously. Concerned and worried about Alex's state of health after his visit to her, she asked her father and brother to check on his welfare. They duly obliged and visited the bandleader's house in Ruislip. After some time during which there was no response to their repeated knocking and ringing at the door, and knowing full well he was indeed at home, they broke in to find him very ill in bed, but still protesting he had no need of a doctor. They immediately called for medical assistance and he was taken to the hospital.

Maggie visited him daily and, on the Sunday at the end of his first week's hospitalisation, she was shocked to be told he had only a week to live. Alex died five days later at 11.45pm on Friday 2nd July, 1982, exactly one week before his fifty-third birthday.

Over the last three decades, Maggie and I have talked many times about his life and death from both our viewpoints, and have decided that, although his life was curtailed, in his relatively short existence on this earth, he experienced more fulfilment in giving and getting both pleasure and joy in life than most would enjoy in two lifetimes.

So, a chapter in my own life came to a close. I had eighteen of the most rewarding, enjoyable, fulfilling years of my existence. There were moments of elation and sadness, euphoria and despair, affluence and poverty, excitement and weariness but, above all, there was camaraderie, friendship, teamwork, and great, great music. I am so glad Alex invited me to *"go and get your guitar. Laddie"* all these years ago.

I wish he could be here to ask me again.

The End

DISCOGRAPHIC

Before I joined the band, Alex had, with the help of 'A and R' manager (artists and repertoire) Denis Preston, issued some classic albums on the Columbia label. 'Dixieland to Duke / Music of the Mauve Decade', 'It's Right Here for You', 'Echoes of Chicago' and 'The Melrose Folio', were well established quality recordings made even better with the addition of stars like Gerry Salisbury, Danny Moss, and Joseph Reinhardt. Some singles featuring Dickie Valentine and the ubiquitous Lennie Hastings, in Teutonic mode, had made their mark in the 'Hit Parade', as had a pretty song by Norrie Paramor called 'Tansy', and a version of Cole Porter's 'Rosalie, I Love You'.

With the reforming of his band involving yours truly, Alex decided to let the chaps find each other and, through time, formulate a new repertoire. When he felt the time was right, after a successful one-off album, 'Blowing Wild', featuring Wild Bill Davison live at the Manchester Sports Guild on the Jazzology label, we went into the studios to record 'Strike One'. The line-up was: Alex, Roy Williams, John Barnes, Fred Hunt, Len Hastings, Ron Mathewson, and myself. Among the tracks, two stand out for me; 'I wished on the Moon', and 'That Old Feeling', which featured some fine bass playing from Ron. It also included 'Bluesology', my first solo recording. An EP, 'Alex Welsh Entertains' was also published from the same session, featuring Dixieland-style tracks. The release of these albums caused quite a stir but, alas, nothing more came from 'Strike'.

We were in Edinburgh for our next and probably the best session on 'Parlophone'. Ex clarinettist and Clyde Valley Stompers bandleader, Pete Kerr, had moved into the production of Scottish and light entertainment music for EMI. On hearing that our band was going to be on tour in Scotland around New Year, 1968, he approached Alex with an idea to produce an album called 'At Home', with Al Gay added to the front line as an aid to the still-recuperating John Barnes and, with Ron Rae on bass, two LPs were issued.

The second was named 'Dixieland Party' and featured a photograph of the band posing at the 100 Club in party hats. Although appearing to be well into the mood, the session was in the morning and what you see in my glass was the remains of my one and only pint. The records sold well and we were invited to make another the following year. The front cover was my idea, and the photo of Alex holding a bottle of champagne with a hastily drawn label proclaiming it was 'Vintage 69' was taken at Acker Bilk's famous Capricorn Club. Once again 'Alex Welsh, 69' sold well, although that was the last we made for Parlophone.

The tours with the visiting American stars brought another series of albums, this time on the Fontana label, organised by trumpeter Terry Brown, and recorded in the studios near Marble Arch in London. The first was 'Jazz Means Hines' already mentioned in the chapter on the great pianist. Bud Freeman followed, involving just the rhythm section, as were two of the next and final five, 'The Tenor of Jazz' featuring Bud, Eddie Lockjaw Davies, Ben Webster, and a fine effort by Eddie Miller, (who was so nervous on the session I had to settle him with a gentlemanly port and brandy before recording), and 'Americans in London', a compilation of tracks by several visitors. Eddie Miller also recorded one with the whole band and there was a nice one with Ben Webster and Bill Coleman, again with the rhythm section. At the time, they were considered very important by the band.

In the early 1970s, Alan Bates, who was forming a new label, Black Lion Records, approached Alex. Over the next decade or thereabouts, several fine albums, both studio recordings and live concerts, were issued including: 'If I had a Talking Picture of You' and 'An Evening with Alex Welsh and Friends' (with George Chisholm, Humphrey Lyttelton and Bruce Turner) volumes one and two, 'Dixieland Party, 'Showcase' volumes one and two, 'Alex Welsh in Concert', and 'Salute to Satchmo' with George, Humph, and Beryl Bryden.

Some of these have been reissued as CDs, as have those of the early bands, on the Lake, Candid, and Jazzology labels. There may be more, watch this space!

Epilogue

A Bomber's Moon

The six-piece human car wash was in full operation, spraying the near side of the Ford Transit mini-bus, which had almost become home to the Alex Welsh Jazz Band. The musicians gazed skywards as the warm urine splashed on the cold metal of the wheels, sending clouds of steam upwards into the starlit, frosty atmosphere.

"It's a bomber's moon tonight, all right!" exclaimed Fred, who, like Lennie, had survived the Blitz as a young man in London.

"Zis time you vill all be smeshed to smizzereens!" replied Herr Hastings, who was still wearing the German tin helmet from the gig.

The others remained silent; too tipsy, or tired, or both to care. In the meantime, the seventh member, the band leader, who hadn't bothered to alight, sat with a bottle in his hand in the front passenger seat.

"Shut the f****** door!" he shouted; "it's bloody freezing!"

Without reply, each member took his appointed seat and the bus set off once more, homeward bound. No one noticed Len's 'Irish' trapped half-in, half-out of the side door. Exposed to the elements, it frequently travelled in this manner, to be rescued, often soaking wet and dirty and slapped on its wearer's head when he was dropped off at his *Reichstag*.

It had been a typical gig. The main topics of conversation on the way to the venue had been England's successful winter tour of India, and the state of the 'date sheet'.

"What's this? Another cancelled tour of Australia?" Lennie had asked, bringing smiles to the faces of five musicians and a scowl to that of the sixth. Unfortunately, we had arrived late as was often the case and, after a frantic setting up of the drums and PA system and grabbing a quick pint at the bar, we were ready to play.

"As Long as I Live!" called Alex, to get things rolling.

"That won't be very long what with all these cancelled tours of Australia!" Adolph Hitler's understudy replied.

"Just get on with it! One, two, one-two-three-four!"

ii

The atmosphere was set. It would be a good night. Band numbers were inter-spaced with featured solos and all the time booze slipped down the throats of the thirsty musicians at an alarming rate. After Fred's piano feature had brought the house down, it was The Fuhrer's turn.

"Anyone got half a crown?"

Resignedly, Alex put his hand in his pocket and parted with a one-way coin (someone once worked out that Lennie got fifteen shillings a week more than the others, to which he had replied that it was his 'sticks and trousers allowance').

Screwing the two-shilling and sixpenny monocle into his right eye, and adopting a Richard Tauber like pose, Herr von Splatz, with a proud sneer, launched into his 'cod' German version of the song, 'Auf Wiedersehen'.

"Zie fish und chips!" crooned Britain's answer to the Hitler Youth Movement, and the performance ended in laughter and applause and shouts of "more" from the audience. They got two choruses of 'Oh, Baby!' and two choruses of 'Sleepy Time Down South', and that was it – to the bar for a latey or two, pack the instruments, load the bus, and off home; typical, but great.

The next day sees the band set off on a four-day tour of North-West England, starting in the sleepy little town of Kendal in the Lake District. Let me state categorically that there are more ravers in Kendal than there in the whole of London and Home Counties put together. Quiet it may seem but, believe me, more livers have been permanently damaged there than anywhere I know, including Scotland.

Travelling time is about four hours of quiet insanity, cricket chat, Scrabble, and packed lunches. Hastings produces his latest gastronomic delight: cheese and garlic on toast, burnt to a frazzle and covered in black pepper. John produces a new cassette recorder, not long on the market, and impromptu interviews and sketches are devised. Sheer lunacy prevails; travel-itis we called it. With about an hour to go, Jim suddenly develops a dry throat, brought on by the dust in the wagon, of all things.

"Aaarrrgghhh," he cries, clutching his throat. The first pint won't touch the sides.

The bus pulls up alongside The County Hotel, where the band is performing and staying that evening. Travel-worn, the chaps file into Reception to pick up room keys. "Oh God; don't tell me I've got to share with Hitler again."

Having dumped his effects, Jim heads for the bar to lubricate his dry throat. Lennie, whose suitcase has already exploded, showering the room with its contents, looks for a betting shop to find out how much he has lost, and will therefore have to sub later that evening. Roy goes to bed, Harvey checks over the engine, John stands on his head in pursuit of his latest fad for yoga, and Fred joins Jim at the bar, while Alex disappears to his room, not to be seen until five minutes before playing time.

iii

The evening has arrived. The room set aside for the performance has been packed since seven o'clock. The local jazz band, led by a fine trumpeter called Les Bull, has already struck up when our heroes enter the arena. Les's band has a good following and will warm the audience nicely. Soon, pints in hands, the chaps take the stand. Alex calls 'Opus One'. The seven-piece band sounds like seventeen and they are off and flying.

Dixieland war-horses, mainstream standards, solos and comedy numbers are all part of the programme. Alex and Fred raise the roof with 'Davenport Blues'. The 'small band within the small band' performs a greatly appreciated 'Open Country'. Meanwhile, Herr Splatz is sinking gin and tonic faster than the Titanic, thinking, no doubt, about his spot and drawing mental inspiration from his two heroes: Hitler and Tauber; a fine double-act! When his moment arrives, he fits the acquired half-crown, dons the tin helmet and, with trousers rolled up to knees, 'cods' his way through 'Auf Wiedersehen' in his familiar throaty tenor voice. Great stuff.

When it is all over, the two bands mingle with guests at the bar. Bill Lambert, our gracious host, has served sandwiches and a round of drinks, and the talk is of the evening's pleasures. Tired but happy, the strolling vagabonds finally hit the sack; tomorrow is another day.

At the crack of lunch the next day, seven under-rested, over-boozed wrecks, having survived the insistent pressure of frustrated chamber maids waiting to "do your room, sir!" and their ultimate weapon, the hoover outside your door, struggle with their luggage to the bus and set off on the next stage of the tour.

It's Blackpool tonight, for the Leonard Cheshire Foundation, and once again the chaps will play and stay in the same hotel, the Fernleaf at St. Anne's. As usual there will be the regular crowd of fans, friends and ear-benders. There was a rule in the band about the latter. As long as the offender was buying drinks while boring the pants off you, it was all right. If no liquid refreshment appeared to be forthcoming, the sufferer would tug gently on one of his ear lobes, a sign to the others that he needed rescuing by a phone call from home or some such ploy. Making his escape, the mauled musician would make sure to avoid the offender for the rest of the evening.

And so the gigs would continue: jazz clubs, private functions or concerts and corporate events, until eventually would come the dreaded last day of the tour. It wasn't the thought of returning home that was so dreadful. Far from it! The last was usually also the longest day. Nerves shot to pieces by excessive boozing and tiredness, the exhausted musicians would find themselves out of their hotel rooms just after the latest possible breakfast, with an hour or so to drive to somewhere like Derby, beckoning. Don't be mistaken, Derby is as nice a city as any, and some of the nicest, keenest jazz *aficionados* live there or thereabouts but, with no hotel to book into, the chaps would find they had several hours to 'lig about', with only pubs or cinemas to pass the time. The pubs, of course, in those anti-social times, closed for several hours in the afternoon, leaving only the pictures and their insistent Norman Wisdoms or 'The Sound of Music'. Uugghh!

iv

Once, however, we were surprised to see a presentation of 'The Naked Prey', a film about the retaliation by African tribesmen against white ivory hunters, starring Cornel Wilde. There wasn't much plot, but the effects were shockingly stunning. We had just come to the end of a tour with Bill Davison at his wildest, and that film destroyed what was left of our jangling nervous system.

But strangely enough, the last gig always invariably turned out to be one of the most enjoyable. Whether it was the thought of returning home, or sheer exhaustion, or a combination of the two, it always turned out to be a relaxed, swinging session.

And, so, a typical tour would come to an end. It seemed hard work at the time and often required tedious hours of travelling, but I personally wish I could do it all again tomorrow, even if it meant another viewing of 'The Sound of Music'!

Looking back, I wouldn't change a thing. It was an unforgettable, joyful experience. Thanks chaps!

Printed in Great Britain
by Amazon.co.uk, Ltd.,
Marston Gate.